GIRLS, GODDESSES & GROWING UP

Susan Highsmith

Words Matter Publishing
P.O. Box 1190
Decatur, IL 62525
www.wordsmatterpublishing.com

ISBN: 978-1-962467-94-0

Library of Congress Catalog Card Number: 2025939630

DEDICATION

I dedicate this book to all girls and women
who are awakening to the Divinity within them.
May all of the qualities of the Divine Feminine
that have been latent come forth
to Grace their lives and all lives
on this precious planet.

TABLE OF CONTENTS

ACKNOWLEDGEMENTS vii

FORWARD ix

GIRLS, DISCOVER THE BEAUTY & TRUTH
OF WHO YOU ARE! 1
  ✧ BEGINNINGS 1
  ✧ LOVE 2
  ✧ PRENATAL & PERINATAL PSYCHOLOGY (PPNP) 13
  ✧ BONDING & ATTACHMENT 22
  ✧ SELF-ESTEEM 27

ARCHETYPES: THE GODDESSES 37
  ✧ PALLAS ATHENA: TRUTH, POWER & PROTECTION 43
  ✧ SOPHIA: WISDOM & ENLIGHTMENT 46
  ✧ THE VIRGIN OF GUADALUPE/MOTHER MARY:
    LOVE & REVERENCE FOR ALL LIFE 51
  ✧ WHITE TARA: THE CORE OF PURITY WITHIN 56
  ✧ IXCHEL: HEALING & INNER VISION 60
  ✧ LADY VENUS: DIVINE GRACE & BEAUTY 63
  ✧ KUAN YIN: MERCY, COMPASSION & FORGIVENESS 68
  ✧ AMATERASU: CLARITY, DIVINE PERCEPTION &
    DISCERNMENT 73

❖ THEMIS: HARMONY, BALANCE, CONFIDENCE & ASSURANCE 76

❖ PAX & LAKSHMI: PEACE & PROSPERITY FOR ALL.......... 82

❖ FREYA: JOY, ENTHUSIASM & DIVINE PURPOSE............... 85

❖ ISIS: TRANSFORMATION 90

❖ MOTHER EARTH, MAWU, GAIA, OSHUN & PACHAMAMA: FEELING MOTHERED, GROUNDED & AT HOME 93

❖ HIDING IN PLAIN SIGHT: IMAGES OF THE DIVINE FEMININE... 98

WHAT'S A GODDESS TO DO? 105

❖ I AM EXPRESSING MY TRUTH & MY POWER 110

❖ I AM ACCESSING MY OWN WISDOM 120

❖ REPROGRAMMING MYSELF 124

❖ I AM LOVING MYSELF 133

❖ I AM RESTORING MY LIFE TO ITS ORIGINAL BLUEPRINT 139

❖ I AM VIBRANTLY HEALTHY 144

❖ I LIVE A GRACE-FILLED LIFE... 154

❖ I FORGIVE MYSELF & OTHERS 157

❖ I CAN SEE CLEARLY NOW 167

❖ I AM BALANCED & HARMONIOUS.................................. 178

❖ PEACE & PROSPERITY ARE MY DIVINE BIRTHRIGHT 186

❖ I AM ON PURPOSE IN MY LIFE WITH JOY & ENTHUSIASM 194

❖ I AM TRANSFORMING MY LIFE 201

EPILOGUE 213

❖ SELF ESTEEM 213

❖ THE TRUTH ABOUT YOU 215

❖ YOU CAN RELAX NOW 216

REFERENCES... 219

ACKNOWLEDGEMENTS

It is a joy to acknowledge my family and friends who have supported me during the writing of this book. They have all continually seen this work being completed, even when I felt my energy flagging. Their encouragement has been invaluable. I especially want to thank my beloved husband for his willingness and unfailing efforts to support me in so many ways. His ability to view my computer as an animate object that he could coax into benevolent service has saved my text more than once. My dear friend Gretchen sent me, unasked-for, beautiful, inspiring books about Goddesses. My spiritual teacher and family at Era of Peace kept me grounded while lifting my vision to see the highest possible outcomes, not just for this book but for humanity and all Life. I am grateful for all the lessons that I have learned ~ and am still learning ~ as I dealt with this sacred subject matter. The awakening of the Divine Feminine needs everyone's acknowledgment. I am graced to share this information in ways that express a lifetime of study, experience, and reflection.

FORWARD

Welcome. Many young women are challenged these days to discover who they are in a patriarchal system that has dominated societies for eons of time. This belief system teaches girls that they are less than, deficient, not good ~ or at least not good enough. The buzzword in therapy seems to be *trauma*, which many women have experienced, and lots of questions are asked, like "What's wrong with you?" That question is slowly changing to "What happened to you?" but the question still suggests that women are victims and are at the mercy of a world they cannot trust. I prefer to ask clients, "What happened?" or "What brings you here?" or "What would you like to work on?"

The idea is to NOT reinforce a self-concept that the individual is damaged and then attempt to make her fit into a paradigm that is itself broken. The idea is to help her develop **self-esteem**, a high regard for herself that transcends the system and gives her new ways to think about herself, fostering the realization of her Divine Potential.

I have been a counselor for over thirty years, evolving through my own process of maturing into a Crone, a Wise Woman who has learned from her own mistakes and wishes to share her hard-won knowledge with the generations that follow. What works, and what errors can be avoided? In my personal search and my academic research, I chose to acquire doctoral degrees in both psychology and Divinity. I felt I needed a college education, *and* God! I hurt and I wanted to find with my body, mind *and* Spirit what I could do to let go of pain and increase my ability to be happy. I wanted to be productive and share what worked for me with my daughter, my granddaughters, and now my great-granddaughter. My heart is happy when I reach out to them and my surrogate daughters around the world, whom I have found through being a volunteer and mentor in organizations I admire.

So, this book is an amalgamation of psychological and Spiritual Wisdom. I talk about God in terms of Father-Mother God. We are all Children of God ~ no child is born without a Father *and* a Mother. Even theologian and social scientist Andrew Greeley stated emphatically in his book *The Mary Myth: On the Femininity of God*:

> In fact, God is both masculine and feminine, and may well have been thought of as a woman long before she/he was ever thought of as male. Primitive humans were convinced that all attributes existed as one in the divinity, and that, therefore, there was every reason to think that both sexes should be more or less clearly expressed together.

In most religions, the accepted view is that God is male and even the Trinity is Father, Son, and Holy Spirit, which has been considered another masculine aspect of the Divine. I have learned that the Trinity is Father God *and* Mother God as well as the Son/Daughter of God. Our Father-Mother God are our God Parents, the Union of the Divine Masculine *and* the Divine Feminine. They represent Divine Fatherhood and Divine Motherhood. These Divine qualities reside within us as children of the Creator/Creatrix.

What has been lost by subjecting half of the world's population to a philosophy that questions everything from whether women can vote to whether women even have Souls? History ~ His Story ~ is full of this questioning. No wonder women seek counseling to help understand their place in a world that often denies that a woman's place even exists.

So, I'll share with you what I have learned, the Truth of my personal experience, my academic studies, and my evolving understanding of the Divine. Please go within your own heart and accept what resonates for you. Let anything else go. If it is meant for you, your Higher Self ~ your own I AM Presence ~ will bring the information to you again and again. No worries. You will get what is right for you at the right time.

Welcome to a different understanding of how we are conditioned during our youth, indeed, from the very beginning of life in the wombs of our mothers. There is a Divine Design for our lives, and there is an ego that has used our Divine Gifts of thought, feeling, and free will to cause us to live according to its design. My intention is to help you discern the difference and become the Best You Can Be.

GIRLS, DISCOVER THE BEAUTY & TRUTH OF WHO YOU ARE!

Where do we begin?

BEGINNINGS

I love puns, and the word *beginnings* could not be better. I have been asking myself how to begin this book, and the whole subject of growing up is deeply rooted in how we each begin - literally, how we start life.

Reflect for a moment: Were you a wanted child, nurtured and loved? Do you feel that Life, specifically your biological parents, welcomed you? Do you feel safe? Can you trust others? Do you expect to be treated well, acknowledged and rewarded for your efforts?

Jeremy Hayward, an author and international education director of Shambhala Training, has said:

> To a very large extent, men and women are a product of how they define themselves. As a result of a combination of innate ideas and the intimate influences of the culture and environment we grow up in, we come to have beliefs about the nature of being human. These beliefs penetrate to a very deep level of our psychosomatic systems, our minds and brains, our nervous

systems, our endocrine systems, and even our blood and sinews. We act, speak, and think according to these deeply held beliefs and belief systems.

When you look at the results in your life today, are you happy and generally satisfied with the way your life is turning out? Are you comfortable economically? Do you have a partner, one who supports you, not just financially, but supports your goals and aspirations? Do you *have* goals and aspirations? Do you have good friends and a social network that you find encouraging and fun? If you have children, are you parenting in ways that give your child what you didn't get, or are you repeating old patterns that will continue a legacy of archaic beliefs and behaviors?

I intend to encourage you to consider those questions in a way that gives you a different perspective, a loving way to hold all the positive *and* negative happenings in your world. My approach is to combine both psychological and spiritual understandings of your experiences so you can find better ways to meet life's challenges.

What we have been overlooking in our culture is how our beginnings shape our lives. We often think that changing others, avoiding them, or railing against them will make a difference. That has not been my experience, although I have certainly tried those strategies. Let's shift our focus to what's really important ~ how we think and feel about ourselves.

Everything about us revolves around our self-esteem. Do we "esteem" ourselves? Do we love ourselves just because? Do we value ourselves? Do we feel worthy, or are we constantly trying to earn love?

LOVE

So, let's talk about love. You may ask, as Tina Turner did in the song, "What's Love Got to Do with It?" The lyrics of this song, written by Graham Lyle and Terry Britten, are quite profound. The real question within the question is, of course, "what's love?"

In our Western English-speaking society, we have only one word for love, and it can mean anything from loving ice cream to loving a person you plan to spend the rest of your life with. Other cultures have many words for love. For example, in Greek, *philia* means affectionate love; *storge* means love without physical attraction, as in love for family members; *eros* means romantic or passionate love; *mania* means obsessive love; *agape* means universal love. The best definition for agape that I know of was given by the founder of SpectraDynamics, Dr. Dorothy Gates. Agape means "giving from yourself from the abundance of having served yourself so well." Dr. Gates' classes were based on the premise that we need to overcome subconscious beliefs of unworthiness and that loving ourselves is essential to having a fulfilling life.

Stuck with only one word in English for love, many of us have been told that we need to love others *unconditionally*. Wow, that has generated more dysfunctional thinking and behavior than we may know. The stories of women behaving like door mats by accepting abuse ~ physical, mental, verbal, and emotional ~ are heard endlessly in counseling sessions, and much of therapy perpetuates victim/blame belief systems. Even religion, the place we go for spiritual assistance and relief, can tell us we were born in "original sin" and, if we don't "love, honor, and obey" our spouses, we are bad, wrong, or not behaving according to God's dictates. "God *is* love" (1 John 4:16) is lost in judgmental thinking, and the phrase becomes a cliché.

In some Middle Eastern cultures women are sequestered, forced to wear burkas, and literally starved or brutalized for any infractions of rules made by the male-dominated religions and institutions in those countries.

We can easily see how society reinforces beliefs that put girls down, makes them less than, and generates thoughts of self-doubt, shame and even self-hatred. Well, here's the crux of the situation. If we grow up believing we are not okay, if we feel unlovable, what are our lives going to look like? Life can be pretty unhappy, unfulfilling and discouraging. It is loving ourselves that is crucial to having a satisfying life.

Let's take a closer look at LOVE. Dictionary.com defines love as

> A set of emotions and behaviors characterized by intimacy, passion, and commitment. It involves care, closeness, protectiveness, attraction, affection, and trust. Many say it's not an emotion in the way we typically understand them, but an essential physiological drive.

This whole definition implies that love is felt for another person. How are we to love ourselves if the very language we use does not even suggest that love of self is normal, desirable or possible? This definition says love is an emotion we can hardly understand, but it is a *drive inherent within us.* If we learn that we can only receive love from another person, we are set up to look for love in all the wrong places! We look for a rescuer who occupies one of the positions on the infamous "victim triangle."

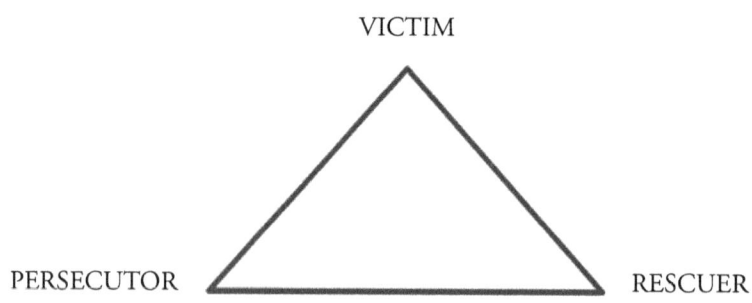

We can spend our lives as a victim, persecutor, or rescuer, often moving from one position to another. Our society indulges victims, which provides a false sense of love for being powerless. We get sympathy and condolences when we are victimized. "Oh, poor you" may feel comforting in the short term, but it does nothing to empower us to claim our divine heritage - a sense of love that reassures us of our right to be loved just because we are born worthy of it.

This faulty belief system encourages us to take care of others first; thus, girls grow up aspiring to be nurses and teachers, honorable careers, giving to others but not necessarily receiving in return. In fact, this creates an imbalance. As our brains develop, new neurons reach out to other neurons to form neural networks. These intersections become depots for similar information. We continually build and reinforce these neural connections so that any other way of thinking seems foreign. We go about our lives "othering," giving love, caring for others, and getting rewarded for putting others first. No circuits in our neural networks are building receivers for love. What love we experience is conditional, based upon our *doing* something, generally for someone else.

If we think of our brain's wiring as an intricate communication system, we can envision it to be comprised of lots of transmitters but few, if any, receivers. Our receptors for love are generally nonexistent or broken! If our networks are jammed with thoughts of othering, we give what we would like to receive, but if love actually shows up, there is no *receiver* for it. We keep looking for love by trying to earn it, to do something to get it, or just accepting ill-treatment or even abuse because we have the idea that is what love looks like and is all we deserve.

What does science have to say about this "essential physiological drive" to have love in our lives? A mentor of mine, cell biologist Bruce Lipton, has concluded from extensive research that human cells have the ability to respond to stimuli in only two ways. If the environment is safe and nurturing, cells will grow; however, if the environment is threatening, cells will protect themselves. They cannot do both at the same time! This responsiveness, according to Dr. Lipton, means that cells are either in a state of love and growth, or in a state of fear and protection.

At the most fundamental level of our physical being we are either in *love* or in *fear*! Love and feelings of safety, trust, openness, and receptivity are synonymous. If our very nature permits only two choices ~ love or fear ~ we must, in order to grow, develop and become our best selves and be *in love*. We must be in love with ourselves or our growth is inhibited.

We must ask ourselves if care was *given* to us or *taken* from us! Did we get the nurturing and safety we required to grow into healthy adults? Most of our beliefs about life, whether we were safe and loved or unsafe and unloved, were instilled so early we could only accept them. The word *in/stilled* has great meaning in this context because it suggests that we were in a state of stillness, open and receptive but not yet able to speak, to articulate a response or even developed enough to ascertain if what was coming into our biocomputer was acceptable or not.

At the very earliest stages of development we simply cannot argue with the information that is bombarding us. Before we are born, in utero, we are growing at a faster rate than we will ever grow again. Our cells are multiplying at an incomprehensible pace, taking in everything in our environment, which includes our mother's mental, emotional, physical and spiritual condition. Was she happy, worried, nervous, relaxed ~ healthy and supported or stressed and alone? Her feelings become our feelings and her beliefs become our beliefs. If she is abused, we learn that abuse is normal. If she is supported and loved we learn that women are worthy and we will expect to be treated with love and respect.

Not only does our mother's well-being make a difference in how we gestated in her womb, and how the developing cells in our bodies were experiencing love or fear, the state of mind of *her* mother also impacted us. Did you know that the egg that became YOU was in your mother's ovary while she was in your grandmother's womb? No wonder it is said that we are affected by the generations that came before us. Biology and psychology are telling us that love is critical for our well-being, but we sabotage love with our individual and societal belief systems, intergenerational patterns of behaviors and the way we talk about love including the words we use to define it.

So, what's love got to do with it? The answer is *everything* ~ especially if we can understand what love really is. We are expressions of love or expressions of fear at the most basic level. Notice in your life when you feel comfortable and safe. Notice those times when you feel insecure and hypervigilant. When you are in a social setting with friends, in a classroom with fellow students, in a business environment with colleagues, in an intimate situation with a close companion ~ your life is all about relationships ~ notice how you feel. Can you trust those you interact with to treat you with respect or are you on guard, fearing that you will be harmed in some way? Memories of abandonment, rejection, betrayal, criticism and more are embedded in the cells of your body. Ann Rothschild has written a book on the subject that emphasizes this truth: *The Body Remembers*!

At the core of your feelings are the cellular memories of how you were first treated and, more importantly, how you perceived that treatment. The intentions of those who raised you matter less than the conclusion you drew from their treatment. A newborn baby being taken away from her mother after spending 100 percent of her life in the body of that person, feels isolated, alone, fearful, perhaps in terror that without her mother she will die. Yet we remove babies from their mothers at birth as if this is the most natural thing in the world. This practice is taken for granted. If we understand cell biology, babies internalize every event as either loving or fearful because the body is an amalgamation of cells, each one responding to input either open to receive or closed to protect itself.

There is more . . . . Ongoing research by clinicians like Dr. John Gottman have studied the chemistry of love. When we are in love we secrete the hormone oxytocin. This neuropeptide is produced in the hypothalamus of our brains and is stored in, and subsequently released from, the posterior pituitary gland. According to Dr. Gottman, oxytocin appears to down-regulate responses. He contends that "oxytocin and vasopressin appear to be the hormones of trust in all relationships." Experiencing love early in life creates patterns of thought and feeling that build the foundation for lifelong health and loving relationships. And these two hormones flow abundantly when a woman gives birth without interventions such as drugs and/or surgery. Oxytocin is literally our first taste of love.

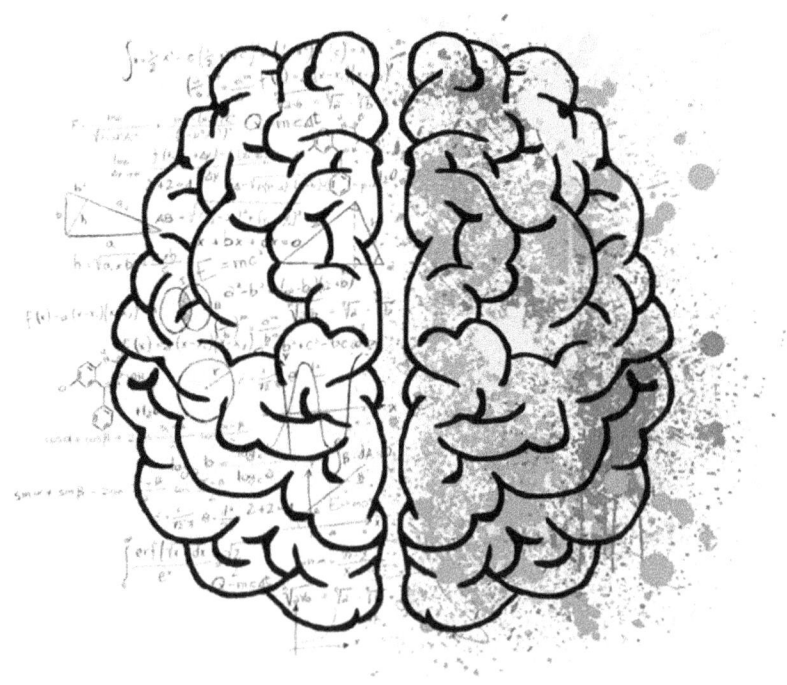

This image depicts our current understanding of the brain. The left hemisphere of our neocortex, the new brain, is tasked with logic, analysis, linear thinking, speech, language processing and the proverbial reading, writing and arithmetic skills ~ those characteristics that are considered masculine. The right brain is responsible for creativity, imagination, artistic abilities, spatial awareness, intuition, holistic thinking, non-verbal memory and emotions ~ those characteristics that are considered feminine. We all need the capabilities of both sides of the brain but the left brain has been celebrated, indeed, acclaimed as masculine and worthy while the right brain has been disparaged as feminine, too emotional and unworthy.

Girls have been identified as members of the weaker sex, being too emotional and, therefore, less rational, and as the objects of sex. Ironically, the essence of being female is being receptive, the receiver of the male's generative power. Women are damned for the very gifts endowed by their Creator who has both Divine Masculine *and* Feminine characteristics.

Let me tie some of these concepts together. As a prenatal and perinatal psychologist I learned about oxytocin in the context of childbearing. Oxytocin is called the *hormone of love*, and it is in abundant supply when a woman is giving birth, as I mentioned earlier. In fact, it was discovered to speed up the birthing process by Sir Henry Dale in 1906. Through relaxation, meditation and hypnosis, women are giving birth with little or no pain ~ and no drugs. These techniques foster the natural release of oxytocin and other birth-enhancing hormones.

Swedish researcher Dr. Kerstin Moberg studied oxytocin and found that its functions extended beyond childbearing, nursing and maternal behaviors. Dr. Moberg urges adults to engage in oxytocin-stimulating activities like yoga and meditation because this hormone has calming effects and promotes social bonding. Oxytocin is a principal ingredient in our internal medicine cabinets and can help maintain lifelong health. It is exciting to learn that this hormone is released during birthing and reduces the need for the common practice of intervening with Pitocin or other artificial drugs that mimic oxytocin but increase pain as they intensify contractions. Dr. Gottman emphasizes that oxytocin downregulates our fear response. Ongoing research is finding that this "cuddle hormone" significantly increases positive behaviors and reduces negative behaviors. Feeling love just feels good!

Love is inextricably entwined in the creative process itself. Love is a principle, a God-given gift to all of humanity. If that is so, it should be dispensed with reverence, and it should start with acknowledgment and appreciation for the gift of life ~ our own. How can we truly love others if we do not love ourselves? Our new beginning starts the moment we discover love for ourselves, the children of the Creative Source, Father-Mother God.

Patricia Cota-Robles, an internationally renowned spiritual teacher and founder of the organization *Era of Peace*, says this about love: "It is an immutable natural Law that in order for us to be capable of Loving any other part of life—any person, place, condition or thing—YOU MUST FIRST LOVE YOURSELF."

Love for ourselves is an insulator that reduces the inclination to protect ourselves. In the song "What's Love Got to Do with It," the lyrics call love a "second-hand emotion" and the dictionary definition that promotes the idea that love only comes from another individual makes us believe that love is not first-hand! We are encouraged to think of love only coming from someone else, certainly not from within ourselves or from our Creative Source. If we are disappointed in love, of course, we would be wary of loving again and very likely unwilling to look for love within ourselves.

The song asks, "Who needs a heart when a heart can be broken?" Having experienced rejection, abandonment, abuse, or neglect as infants, we have been primed to shut down our hearts and avoid love. Yet this denial is costly. The greatest cause of death in the

United States is heart disease. What are heart attacks? They are broken hearts. Our language, and our songs, aptly identify exactly what we do to ourselves when others betray our trust. We close down and literally harden our hearts. We learned this when we were so little that we only had instinctive organic responses to demonstrate our distress. If our cries went unheeded, our voice was silenced and we may choose not make an effort to be heard. Why bother?

The autonomic nervous system is our anatomical pathway for responding. Once programmed, as early as in utero, and certainly during childhood, we tend to respond the same way again ~ and again ~ and again. The patterns first established in our bodies and minds continue to play out just like recordings on your CD player, computer, phone or other electronic devise you listen to over and over.

Love is an energy universally thought of as centered in our hearts. The HeartMath© Institute has been researching heart energy for decades. They have developed a diagram that depicts our heart fields and tell us that our fields connect. Whenever you are in the presence of another person, your heart fields will overlap. If you begin to think of yourself as an energy being ~ vibrating atoms, electrons, and swirling particles and waves of energy ~ this begins to make sense.

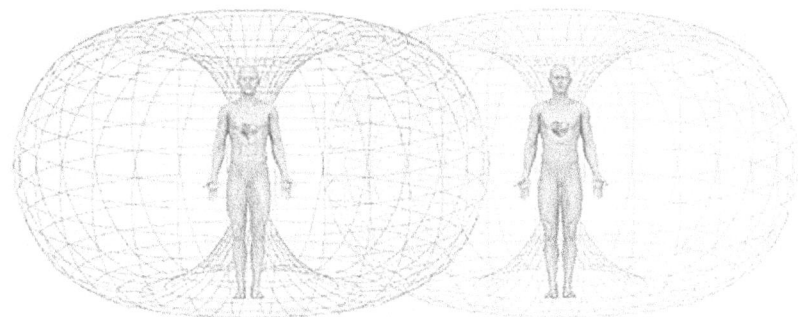

Heartmath.org

11

If you are intuitive or sensitive to energies, you may experience being in someone's "field." This is a field of energy shaped like a donut, called a torus. It cannot be seen with our naked eyes but its vibrations can be measured. You may be able to discern another's field for yourself. A stranger sitting next to you in a movie theater might evoke negative feelings and you may decide to move to another seat. A dear friend might evoke warmth, friendship and a genuine desire to move closer, to hug. In this case your heart fields are resonating positively. They are in tune with one another.

What is most desirable is to sense your own heart field and bring it into coherence, the word that the HeartMath© Institute uses for the state that expresses optimal Heart Rate Variability. When we are coherent our cells are open, our hearts are open, and we are radiating positive, loving energy to the world around us. We might even feel the bliss of loving ourselves.

In making a case for Loving ourselves, I have been defining love in scientific, biological, psychological and spiritual terms. The great avatars spoke of loving ourselves. The Buddha said, "You, yourself, as much as anybody in the entire universe, deserve your love and affection." Jesus said, "Love your neighbor as yourself. "As" means while, at the same time as. We are reminded to love ourselves in the same way we love others. Again, how can we truly love others if we don't first love ourselves?

David Hawkins, psychiatrist and founder of the Institute for Spiritual Research, has called loving "a state of being . . . that emanates from the heart." He says, "Love is misunderstood to be an emotion; actually, it is a state of awareness, a way of being in the world, a way of seeing oneself and others." This expands our notion of love beyond an emotion or the trite way that many think about love as simply a physical attraction or a self-sacrificing compulsion to deny ourselves the very love we are giving away. Love is an energy, a vibration, a state of consciousness. Awakening our consciousness to love as an inherent aspect of ourselves opens our hearts and minds to our own Divinity.

Love. What's your definition? When you think about love do you send loving thoughts to yourself? Is your self-talk filled with positive affirmations about how lovable, how beautiful, how good you are? If not, stay tuned for what to do about Love.

PRENATAL & PERINATAL PSYCHOLOGY (PPNP)

This branch of psychology has been around for a century but is still not widely known. In 2004, two of my colleagues at Santa Barbara Graduate Institute collaborated with me to produce a 21-minute DVD we titled *Babies Know: Seven Principles of Prenatal & Perinatal Psychology*. It is still in use and has been distributed around the globe. Carol Landsberg, Mary Anne Vernallis and I defined PPNP this way:

The field of Prenatal and Perinatal Psychology is dedicated to demonstrating, through research, education and therapy, a reverence for human life that encompasses preconception, gestation, birth and the early postnatal period. Prenatal and Perinatal Psychology is a multidisciplinary approach that explores in depth the biological, psychological, mental, emotional, and social development of babies as they grow into unique individuals through their relationships with caregivers. It honors the essence of life throughout the entire lifespan, and emphasizes the significance of the earliest formative relationships, which create the foundation for all subsequent interactions with others.

What's significant about this field of psychology is that it recognizes the period of human development *before* birth and the period *before* the age of three. Traditional psychologists and psychiatrists have long held the view that people could not remember events in their lives before the age of three, therefore, those events could not affect their adult lives. PPNP has revealed that this assertion is absolutely NOT true.

Studies of trauma have substantiated the PPNP premise that from the moment of conception memories are formed and influence the trajectory of a person's life. However, trauma theory was thought to be strictly a psychological phenomenon. Dr. Thomas Verny, well-known author of *The Secret Life of the Unborn Child* (1981), has now published *The Embodied Mind* (2021) in which he states that the effects of trauma impact children on a biological level as well. Dr. Verny's *embodied mind* is a mind that transcends the physical brain which is confined to the skull. It is a body-wide system containing subconscious memories held at a somatic level that can be triggered regardless of what can be recalled, or not, on a conscious level.

Dr. Verny states that the genetic information held in a fertilized human egg contains the architectural blueprint for building a body and also "may include data reflecting experiences and personality characteristics of the parents." To our genetic inheritance we now add the effects of the environment and experience which also impact our development. Beyond-the-gene thinking represents the science of epigenetics. Epigenetics refers to those external influences that turn genes on, so it is generally acknowledged today that *we are not victims of our genes*. Environmental conditions including the thoughts, beliefs, feelings and actions of those around us contribute to the activation of genes. The Center on the Developing Child at Harvard University states: "What surrounds us, shapes us. In 2024, our work underscored how experiences and exposures in children's developmental environments affect not only their development but also their lifelong health and well-being." This idea acknowledges both Nature (genes) and Nurture (environment) as contributors to the way we turn out.

In a previous book, *Pre-Parenting: Nurturing Your Child from Conception,* Dr. Verny (2002) said that during gestation a baby's brain is organized. "Every biological process leaves a psychological imprint, and every psychological event changes the architecture of the brain. In short, early experience largely determines the architecture of the brain and the nature and extent of adult capacities." He notes that "from the moment of conception, the experience in the womb shapes the brain and lays the groundwork for personality, emotional temperament and the power of higher thought." The word psychological implies even more ‑ psyche + logical ‑ that is, the soul/spirit (psyche) plus the mind (logical).

The conceptus starts accepting information immediately and continues to do so throughout gestation. The 10 months (an ideal pregnancy lasts 280 days, 40 weeks or 10 months according to the March of Dimes) of pregnancy is a vital part of development, indeed, the most important period of development as it establishes the foundation for how life will be lived. Whatever we first experience becomes our *normal.*

Whether we are loved or abused, lavished with attention or neglected, becomes the model for how we expect the world to be. We form expectations that the world will treat us the same way in the future as we have been treated in the past. Once those patterns are initiated in our brain/body architecture, they are hard to change. The longer the patterns persist, the harder the job will be to change them.

In a distillation of the principles that underlie prenatal and perinatal psychology, the aforementioned DVD *Babies Know* synthesizes those concepts that are simple and most relevant to our understanding of this discipline:

1. Conception, pregnancy and birth are natural processes.
2. Pregnant mothers and babies share experiences.
3. Babies are conscious, aware and expressive.
4. Babies need loving support for optimal development.
5. Babies' first relationships lay the foundation for all relationships.
6. Experience dramatically affects the development of babies' brains.
7. Imprints from early experiences can be enhanced—or transformed at any time.

Psychologist David Chamberlain, a pioneer in the field of prenatal psychology, said during his interview and shared in the DVD *Babies Know*:

> Prenatal and perinatal psychology is a new science about the first stages of human development ~ the very first ~ from before conception to a little after the birth. . . . The influence, the love or the hostility, and the nourishment or the starvation that the mother and father provide to this baby growing in the womb affect how the baby can grow and how the brain can develop. It's prenatal psychology as we see it because we think the psyche of the baby is very much alive. We have lots of evidence to show that, but people don't know it yet and we need to talk about it constantly to get people to open the womb and let them peek inside and be able to redefine in their own mind what a baby is. Then it's not something wooden; it's not inert; it's not passive; it's not a passenger in the womb. It is a participant in the womb. It's part of everything the mother is doing. . . . The baby is never without awareness and consciousness.

You were a baby once. How were you treated?

Prenatal and perinatal psychology encompasses many disciplines and emphasizes the importance of physical as well as psychological development. Before we consider the emergence of self-esteem (love for self), we need to look at how the brain is developing in utero. From a single cell to the vast amalgamation of neurons with their hundreds of thousands of connections in the brain, it has been observed that this intricate system is evolving at an exponential pace. Three weeks after conception a baby's heart begins to beat revealing that brain and heart have been growing in tandem. The heart is embraced by the neural tube, the first primitive structure of the forming brain. This process has a guidance system of its own. Mother is not consciously dictating how this happens step-by-step, but her thoughts and feelings are impacting the development of this new intelligence.

The Triune Brain Theory is an easy way to understand brain development but it has been superseded by the Adaptive Brain Theory which is a more current and accurate way to talk about the brain. For ease, let's consider the three-part brain but acknowledge that the systems work together and are interconnected, interrelated and interdependent.

The brain stem is also known as the Reptilian Brain, R-complex, Lizard Brain, Dinosaur Brain or Primal Brain. This oldest part of the brain in evolutionary terms is survival-oriented. It is comprised of the midbrain, pons and medulla oblongata. *ScienceDirect* tells us that "this brain layer does not learn very well from experience but is inclined to repeat instinctual behaviors over and over in a fixed way. In humans, this part of the brain controls survival activities like breathing, heart rate, and balance." The Reptilian brain is an either/or system. It functions like a single cell, growing or protecting baby with fight/flight/freeze responses ~ in love or fear. It's important to know that the survival brain is resistant to change because, when we discuss making changes later, we can anticipate encountering resistance and, indeed, sabotage to our efforts.

The part of the brain that sits on top of the Reptilian Brain is called the Limbic Brain. Essential glands make up this complex system including the basal ganglia, cerebrum, thalamus and hypothalamus, hippocampus, pineal gland, pituitary gland, cerebellum and the infamous amygdala.

WebMD says:

> The primary limbic system function is to process and regulate emotion and memory while also dealing with sexual stimulation and learning. Behavior, motivation, long-term memory, and our sense of smell also relate to the limbic system and its sphere of influence.

The largest part of the triune brain is the Neocortex. This word means new layer. It has four lobes: the frontal, temporal, parietal and occipital. It is also divided into the right and left hemispheres which provide cognitive and intuitive abilities that far exceed those of other mammals. According to Paul MacLean's Triune Brain Theory, these three areas of the brain have unique responsibilities for thinking (neocortex), feeling (limbic brain) and acting (reptilian brain). Some, like Joseph Chilton Pearce who wrote *Evolution's End*, think the prefrontal cortex is a fourth brain because it is considered our executive center with connections to many other parts of the brain. Dan Siegel (1999), author of *The Developing Mind,* says the prefrontal cortex is "central to the process of creating meaning and emotion and enabling flexibility of response."

The brain is enclosed in a skull unable to receive information directly from the outside world. Brains have extensions that allow them to receive input from multiple sources. There are two eyes on stalks that permit the brain to see; two ears on either side of the head that allow it to hear sounds; a nose with two nostrils for smelling aromas; a mouth that tastes food and beverages, and also permits speech; and finally, the skin, the same tissue that embryologically evolved into the brain, takes in data through its ability to respond to tactile sensations. The brain has a voracious appetite. It wants data ~ more input! But it processes that data on the basis of what it has acquired before. Does the information agree or disagree with past experience? Even when new information disagrees with old beliefs, the statement it could make might be, "don't confuse me with the facts; my mind is made up!" Have you ever listened to someone whose mind is made up? This inflexible thinking forms habits of behavior, and the more entrenched the thoughts, emotions or actions, the harder they are to change.

New research has shown that the brain might better be understood as adaptive. Rather than parts of the brain working independently, the journal *Frontiers in Psychiatry* (2022) reports:

The brain appears to work by integrating interoceptive and exteroceptive information to make predictions about future metabolic, energy, and other needs while it adapts to continually changing external and internal conditions to maintain homeostasis and to initiate allostasis as needed.

This ability to adapt is particularly relevant in our modern society due to the amount of stress we experience. We biologically and psychologically tend to want things to stay the same (homeostasis), but conditions may require changes or adaptations to new circumstances (allostasis).

Stephen Porges has developed the Polyvagal Theory which focuses on the tenth cranial nerve, the vagus nerve, also known as the wanderer. This is the only nerve that exits the head and travels (wanders) throughout the body. Porges titled his article published by the National Institutes of Health, *The Polyvagal Theory: New insights into adaptive reactions of the autonomic nervous system.*

Researchers like Porges recognize the adaptability of the brain and nervous system.

We have all heard of fight or flight. These are responses of our autonomic nervous system (ANS), but they are not the only two possibilities. The range of possibilities has evolved as our brains have evolved and adapted to life's challenges. When we are frightened, threatened or stressed in ways that activate our internal coping mechanisms, we go first to our *social engagement system* to communicate with another for empathy, comfort or love. Unfortunately, many of us, as children, never got appropriate responses to our distress. Too often our cries were dismissed as unimportant, ignored or punished. The refrain, "Stop crying or I'll really give you something to cry about" is all too familiar.

When no one reassures a child, she can feel betrayed, not worth an adult's time and effort. In those moments the seeds of unworthiness are sown and beliefs like "I'm not safe," "No one loves me," "I can't trust anyone" "I must be bad because no one is helping me" begin to fester at a deeply subconscious level. Nevertheless, the physiological mechanisms have already gotten the message. So when afraid again, the social system and the desire to engage with another person who can alleviate our distress are bypassed.

We then go to the next facet of our ANS, the *sympathetic nervous system* (SNS). Most of us have a default response so that we either want to run away (flight) or argue and contend physically (fight). Sometimes we actually run, or we threaten to run away. Sometimes we might strike or threaten to hit another person. At times we might actually leave, but we take our issues with us so it is likely that we would encounter a similar situation in the future. These are coping mechanisms but not solutions to the underlying patterns that create the problems in the first place.

If these strategies don't work, we rely on the third part of this system, the *parasympathetic nervous system* (PNS). This response involves withdrawing, becoming immobile and dissociating which are freeze responses. The belief that "I have to be alone" can grow so that social engagement becomes difficult, if not impossible.

The amygdala, the part of our brain that is associated with our emotions, is always on the alert for danger. We will respond to threats to our survival, no longer saber tooth tigers but stressful situations in modern life, with whatever tools that have worked in the past, usually fight, flight, or freeze.

John Chitty of the Colorado School of Energy Studies has explained our responses to threats:

> We play our newest, best card first, [the social engagement system] if that doesn't work (or has not worked in the past as determined by the amygdala), we try our older, second card [the sympathetic nervous system]. If that doesn't work, we play our oldest, last card [the parasympathetic nervous system]. If that doesn't work we are in extreme danger of death.

Whatever our beliefs, they are programs recorded in our brains, bodies and nervous systems. They do not *want* to change. They are familiar. They were the thoughts, emotions and physical sensations we had when we survived early challenges. These are well-myelinated pathways in our brains. If we give them up we think we won't be safe and could even die.

When we feel helpless or worthless ~ whatever we felt when we were rejected, neglected or abused ~ it's scary. The irony is we keep expecting the same treatment so we can keep feeling the same way we have always felt. We can be used to feeling uncomfortable and miss the discomfort if it's gone. Einstein is credited with saying that doing the same thing over and over again expecting different results is *insanity*! Yet, we do this all the time as we respond to challenges in our lives. We need new programs to replace our old fear-based conditioning. Those are new possibilities that we'll be talking about later.

BONDING & ATTACHMENT

Applications of Love in the context of prenatal and perinatal psychology are found in the subjects of Bonding and Attachment. My favorite definition of bonding was created by Marshall and Phyllis Klaus together with John Kennell in their 1995 book *Bonding: Building the Foundations of Secure Attachment and Independence*. They said that a bond is the tie from an adult to a child. A bond is "a unique relationship between two people that is specific and endures through time." Bonding is falling in love with your baby! How beautiful.

Although the terms bonding and attachment have been used interchangeably, I prefer to keep the two concepts separate to eliminate possible confusion. Attachment is the tie from the infant to the adult, typically the parent. We all attach, that is, we develop relationships that are secure or insecure. Attachment is a style of relating; it is not a diagnosis. As we learn more about attachment, we can evaluate the ways in which we are relating to others and make changes if we decide that we can improve the quality of our relationships.

Attachment can be a confusing word as it is used in spiritual ways to describe clinging to worldly matters. Detachment is encouraged in favor of developing a closer relationship with one's Higher Power.

To stick with the psychological term, attachment is a process that is natural for all humans. Over time, as I have made presentations on this subject, I have found that referring to phrases from transactional analysis enhances the comprehension of secure and insecure attachment. This chart might make it easier to understand a more complex notion. Books and articles abound on attachment theory, but here is a simple way to grasp the basic concepts.

SECURE (55%)	I'M OK AND SO ARE YOU.
AVOIDANT (20%)	I'M OK BUT YOU'RE NOT.
AMBIVALENT (15%)	YOU'RE OK BUT I'M NOT.
DISORGANIZED (10%)	I'M NOT OK AND NEITHER ARE YOU.

To explain a bit more, secure attachment is an ideal in that a person feels good about herself and is tolerant and accepting of others. It is estimated that approximately 55 percent of people in our society have a secure attachment style, but I think that estimate is too high.

Attachment is about *connecting* with others as well as about *exploring*. A secure child will look for a parent or caregiver to assure herself that she is safe and protected, but she can feel comfortable moving away and exploring the world too. My husband was traveling with me and saw a father with his child of three or four walking in a garden. The child leaned over to smell a flower and discovered a bee in a blossom. She looked back at Dad for reassurance which is exactly what children do as they begin to take steps away from their primary caregiver. The father was relaxed and reassuring from a distance, letting the child know that she could continue to sniff the flower, and soon the bee flew away. Panicked parents might have let their own fear scare the child and the episode could have become a traumatic one which instilled a fear of nature that would have remained imprinted in this child for years.

A child who is securely attached both connects with others and explores on her own; she finds life predictable, not frightening or worrisome. As an adult a secure individual appears trusting. They can be objective in assessing situations. When they respond to questions on an Adult Attachment Interview (AAI), their narratives are coherent suggesting that they can access both sides of their brains. They can be logical (left brain) as well as intuitive (right brain).

About 20 percent of people are estimated to be avoidant, also known as detached or dismissing. These people tend to push others away. As a child they tend to be unemotional and may lean away when approached for a hug even by their primary caregiver. Adults who are dismissing appear insensitive, even neglectful. When they respond to questions on the AAI, their narratives are brief and not particularly coherent.

Approximately 15 percent of people in our society are thought to be ambivalent. Children with this style of relating are often wary, and can be passive or act out. Some are very clingy. To the child, due to the way in which caregivers have treated her, she finds life unpredictable. Care was provided sometimes, but not others. A gesture that can be associated with this attachment style is beckoning with one hand while pushing away with the other. An adult with this preoccupied attachment style focuses on the past. Their AAI narratives are long and incoherent. They might jump from describing one experience to another, unable to focus on telling a consistent story.

The remaining ten present of individuals have been identified as disorganized. Children in orphanages have exhibited this confused behavior. A child might freeze or appear dazed. As an adult a disorganized person seems delusional and the underlying trauma in this person's life is unresolved.

Again, these categories are not diagnoses. They are ways to think about interactions and what can be done to overcome childhood conditioning that negatively affects adult relationships. If a child is mistreated, abused or even has witnessed abuse, she may carry her belief that abuse of women is normal into adulthood and unwittingly enter into an abusive relationship.

It may seem normal although her conscious mind says she does not merit maltreatment. On a subconscious level, the pattern was imprinted early and reinforced over time. Once recognized, it can be changed.

We can earn secure attachment! This is actually called *earned secure attachment.* It takes some effort and frequently requires help from a good therapist to overcome old programming; but it is programming that creates dysfunctional thinking, feeling and behavior! Insecure attachment is a *learned* way of relating to others. Our egos, however, like to keep doing what they learned to do so our self-talk, our behaviors and emotions can interfere with our conscious desire to change. We were frightened during our early development and our egos expect that we need to be on guard to avoid being hurt or frightened again. Then we get to be *right* because what we expect tends to happen.

Allan Schore, who wrote *Affect Regulation and the Origin of the Self* (2003), has this to say:

> The idea is that we are born to form attachments, that our brains are physically wired to develop in tandem with another's through emotional communication, beginning before words are spoken. If these things go awry, you're going to have seeds of psychological problems, of difficulty coping, stress in human relations, substance abuse, those sorts of problems later on.

Our earliest memories are implicit, that is, not remembered on a conscious level. Later, when we have a more developed neocortex and have begun to use words to express ourselves, our memories are explicit. I can explicitly recall what I had for lunch today but remembering what happened when I was 18 months old is held implicitly in my subconscious mind and is hard to access. My mother has told me about some episodes from that period of time in my life, but I cannot recall them on a conscious level. However, I have a bodily *felt sense* of some traumatic events that occurred that early. Dr. Schore explains that,

> Attachment strategies, including their defensive and conflicted components, are examples of the non-conscious, implicit, or procedural representations that are developed in infancy before the explicit memory system associated with consciously recalled images or symbols is available.

More simply, the way in which we deal with others is based on hidden memories of interactions that happened before our brains developed the ability to consciously recall them. A behavioral research specialist at the National Institutes of Health has found that "the quality of a child's original attachment still predicts a child's competence, the way they interact with other people, how they do in school, whether they have behavior problems, and on and on."

If this whole subject is new to you, you might be starting to understand that there are things about you that reflect the beliefs of others, particularly those of your parents or primary caregivers. Just to give you an example from my own life, picture me, Susan, in the kitchen with my mother and my eight-year-old daughter baking pies for Thanksgiving. My daughter, Kristi, reaches into the pie dough and takes out a handful of dough and starts to eat it. I get excited and sharply reprimand her saying, "Don't eat that, Kristi. It will give you worms!" My mother laughs out loud and asks: "Where in Heaven's name did you learn that?" I reply, "From you. You taught me that." Mom laughs and says, "I just told you that to keep you out of the pie dough!" I was teaching my daughter what I believed ~ and it wasn't true! Many of our beliefs, prejudices, biases and opinions are based on what we picked up as we grew up and are simply *not true*!

SELF-ESTEEM

The overwhelming, underlying factor in every failure, every challenge, every painful experience we are enduring is a deep-seated, ingrained belief of unworthiness and low self-esteem. Most of us intellectually desire it, but deep inside we don't really believe we will ever experience it.

Patricia Cota-Robles stated that in her book *Stargate of the Heart.* Sanford and Donovan said self-esteem "increases our chance of finding happiness in life and makes it possible to cope with life's disappointments and changes. We need self-esteem because nothing is as important to psychological well-being."

Esteem means respect. If you listen to the amount of self-deprecating humor and the number of times you hear "I'm sorry" when no apology is necessary, you can tell that many people do not respect themselves. Using phrases like "I am worth it," or "I love myself" are not just discouraged in society, but scorned. There are old adages telling us it is good to humble a child because they could grow up to be selfish and arrogant. "Spare the rod and spoil the child" has been uttered often to suggest that children need to be physically disciplined, even whipped or beaten, to keep them from being spoiled. Daniel Siegel told us during his *Babies Know* interview: "You can't spoil a child under 12 months of age." To me, spoiling a child of any age means just the opposite of what society thinks it means. To me spoiling a child implies that her sense of worthiness is being damaged by abuse (using the rod), neglect or other ways in which her self-esteem is negated, damaged, or discouraged. It can be undermined by being associated with how well she performs.

Our language demeans expressions which suggest that we have high regard for ourselves. To esteem means to revere ~ to hold sacred. Self-esteem is often thought of as self-confidence, but is much more than that. We can be confident in our abilities to do certain tasks but still feel we are lacking in other areas. To esteem ourselves is to *know* at the deepest level of our being that we are worthy of love. When we know that, we attract goodness into every aspect of our lives.

Teacher, psychologist and counselor Dorothy Corkille Briggs wrote *Your Child's Self-Esteem: The Key to Life* in 1970. Over fifty years ago she told parents that if their child

> has *high self-esteem*; he has it made. Mounting research shows that the fully functioning child (or adult) is different from the person who flounders through life. The difference lies in his attitude toward himself, his degree of self-esteem.

She explained:

> *High self-esteem is not a noisy conceit.* It is a quiet sense of self-respect, a feeling of self-worth. When you have it deep inside, you're glad you're you. Conceit is but whitewash to cover low self-esteem. With high self-esteem you don't waste time and energy impressing others; you already know you have value.

Briggs succinctly states: *"Self-esteem is the mainspring that slates every child for success or failure as a human being."* It arises *"from the quality of the relationships that exist between the child and those who play a significant role in his life."*

We now know that self-esteem begins in the womb! Not only is our body developing, so is our brain/mind. Our egos are forming based on the experiences we have, and once formed, egos do *not* like to change. Unfortunately, we are subjected to the misperceptions and distorted beliefs of others, particularly our parents and other significant authority figures in our environment. If our father is not in the picture, his absence can be interpreted by a pregnant mom to mean that she is not loved or supported. Those perceptions, thoughts and feelings are impressed on the developing biology and psychology of the child she carries in her womb. Her beliefs become the prenate's beliefs, so the world is seen as one in which men do not show up. It would be challenging for a girl to attract lasting love from a partner if her underlying program is embedded with "men leave me" messages.

Further, if father departs, whether by choice or by death, during a child's early years, the internalized program can become *the man I love most leaves me*. My son died at age 42, leaving his three daughters with this program. Each of my granddaughters has dealt with relationship issues due to this belief and have each, blessedly, worked to overcome this inadvertently acquired programming.

Self-esteem is your self-image. It is the picture you carry around like an ID card within your mind. You could be identifying with aspects of yourself from your past, like an abused or neglected infant, a hurt child, or a teased schoolgirl. This is because your self-image is formed unconsciously by past experiences, triumphs, successes, failures, and humiliations ~ the way others accepted or rejected you from the very beginning.

A teacher I studied with for decades, Dr. Dorothy Gates, said,

No factor is more decisive in psychological development and motivation than the estimate you place on yourself. It is not a conscious judgment. It is difficult to isolate. It is part of every other feeling. It is involved in every emotional response.

Your self-image ~ your self-evaluation ~ is the single most significant key to your behavior. Again, it is formed as a result of how others treated you! You can begin to question your image of yourself by reflecting on how you grew up. Did you grow up with love and acceptance, or rejection and criticism ~ or some combination of both? The major difference between growing up in *love* (acceptance) or in *fear* (disapproval) are the messages we internalize, the beliefs we form about ourselves. Based on how we are treated, and how we see others treated, we form opinions about how the world works, and how we fit into it. Are we safe? Must we constantly find ways to please others? Can we trust other people? Are we worthy of *love*?

Briggs declares we must grow up with two main convictions: "I am lovable (I matter and have value because I exist); and I am worthwhile. (I can handle myself and my environment with competence. I know I have something to offer others.)"

In her Progressive SpectraDynamics seminars, Dr. Dorothy Gates presented three main tasks in a person's life: to first learn in infancy, through the love of others, a sense of **worthiness**; in early childhood and when socializing with peers, a sense of **belonging**; and finally, in adolescence and early adulthood, a sense of **competence**. These qualities build on each other. Damage to the underlying structure of our self-esteem diminishes our judgment of ourselves and compromises our ability to live a fully functioning and purposeful life.

To quickly review: While a baby's brain is developing, so are the cranial nerves. The vagus nerve, known as the "wanderer" carries information between the body and the brain. This two-way nervous (communication) system has three ways of interacting with others: our first response is to communicate with love and empathy; if that fails we will react by fighting or fleeing; our last mode is the oldest evolutionarily and we will collapse or dissociate, unable to cope ~ we are then in danger of dying.

Bruce Lipton, cell biologist, has said, "The music is laid down in the womb; the lyrics are added later." That is a poetic way of saying that imprints are being laid down in utero. We express those impressions verbally when we learn to speak. We, as adults, are behaving out of programs that were recorded in our brains, minds and bodies during our development in the womb and during our childhoods.

The kitten I've included here might be thinking about who she is and how she envisions herself. In the best of all possible worlds, she might imagine herself to be a powerful lioness, the queen of all she surveys.

The author of *The Psychology of Self-Esteem*, Nathaniel Brandon, has said, "To know one is worthy of happiness is the essence of self-esteem." To be happy is to feel safe and loved. Further, the degree to which you felt loved and valued determines today how you care for yourself and how others care for you.

Psychoanalytic psychotherapist Sue Gerhardt proffered in her book *Why Love Matters: How Affection Shapes a Baby's Brain* the degree to which the adults of tomorrow "felt loved and valued" will determine how we, and our earth, will be cared for in the future. She explains that brain development is a use-it-or-lose-it process. Gerhardt describes this process, saying:

The brain keeps what is useful and lets go of the surplus connections that are not going to be needed for this particular life. Out of the chaotic overproduction of connections within the brain, patterns start to emerge. The most frequent and repetitive experiences start to form well-trodden pathways, whilst those connections that lie unused begin to be pruned away. The brain takes shape.

This exquisite process leads to our brains holding on to ideas that get reinforced over time. Negative treatment by caregivers can get impressed while positive treatment, which might occur only infrequently, does not get impressed at all, meaning that later in life a person is only processing negativity and is not able to handle loving treatment when it appears.

Let's go over how we each think of any idea. We all have images stored in our brains/biocomputers. For example, when you think of an idea, there is an image in your mind that is associated with that idea. That image is connected to an attitude. A belief is an idea, a perception, but it can become very strong. Beliefs are how we make sense of the world, how we normalize our experiences and explain how we think the world *is*, as well as who we think we are. Our beliefs become our reality. They are the lens through which we see the world. Here's a diagram of what that process looks like.

IDEA ⟹ IMAGE ⟹ ATTITUDE

Let's consider SNOW. When I say the word "snow" it conjures up an image in your mind. If you love snow you might be envisioning catching a snowflake on your tongue, lying on your back in the snow making a snow angel with your arms, or ice skating on a frozen pond. On the other hand, if you hate snow you might be thinking that it's cold, you fell shoveling snow, or you can't wait to move to a place where it is warm year-round. Your beliefs about snow are unique to you. Once you retrieve an image about any subject, you project an attitude. In a conversation with a friend you might tell them you love snow and are planning a winter holiday. Or, you might tell them all about the injury you sustained skiing and how you will never go to snow country again.

Remember the story I told you earlier about baking pies with my mother and my daughter? That is a perfect example of believing something we are told as a child, even just once. When beliefs are repeated and repeated, they become even stronger. Prejudices, biases and intolerance for those who have different beliefs take hold, having been demonstrated by the adult authority figures in our lives; and they are difficult to change. If we hold images in our subconscious mind that we are not loveable or worthy, when someone says "I love you," there is no neural net to catch it. In fact, we will disagree and, either in words or in the hidden recesses of our mind, we will tell ourselves it is not true. They can't possibly mean it! The message does not agree with the internal image. How tragic!

IDEA   ⟹   IMAGE   ⟹   ATTITUDE
I LOVE YOU.   I'M NOT LOVABLE.   I DON'T BELIEVE YOU.

It is my contention that our receivers are broken. Our beliefs are our perceptions. We have concluded that we were unlovable because we were neglected, abused or criticized, but our inherent lovability is still within us. It is now our job to *know* that and let go of, even transmute, the old programming and become our Highest and Best Self.

Every child thinks that everyone else's family is like theirs. Whatever our circumstances, we will tell ourselves *rational lies* to accept our situation. Abuse can become taken for granted and thought of as just the way adults behave. It can be rationalized that all big people behave violently or that all parents yell at their children. When we learn that this is not true, it can be shocking. Parents often parent the same way they were parented. Thus, beliefs and behaviors pass from one generation to another, each new generation telling itself that this is the way things are. This *my-beliefs-are-better-than-your-beliefs* keeps us separated and at war with others who do not hold the same beliefs we do.

Our beliefs do not just emerge when we are three years old and able to express ourselves in words. They begin at the moment of our conception. Wendy Anne McCarty, professor and author of *Welcoming Consciousness*, says "Our core patterns are established during prenatal-perinatal experience." A baby's brain is an amalgamation of cells (neurons). When the baby is born the brain stem (the reptilian brain) is on line. This primitive part of the brain predominates for the first year while the baby's emotional brain, known as the limbic brain, is developing. The cognitive brain, the neocortex, develops later over years as we grow. A fetus, a baby, and a young child are in a receptive brain wave state that makes them highly suggestible. Babies are like little sponges, taking in everything ~ true or not!

We have all had our patterns of thinking and feeling imprinted in our developing bodies and minds, first by our parents, and also by grandparents, doctors, teachers, ministers and other authority figures. Children view these God-like adults as all-knowing. If a child is reprimanded, disciplined, neglected, abandoned or otherwise mistreated, she thinks there is something wrong with herself. You may have heard many adults share their beliefs which deny their worthiness. It may be time for you to reevaluate your beliefs to determine if they are really yours, and if they are true for you. When we become more self-aware and we begin to understand that we have been shaped by factors outside ourselves, we can take back our power to shed old flawed beliefs and *truly love ourselves.*

Cogent Infotech has looked at "The Impact of Social Conditioning on Women's Leadership" and defines social conditioning like this:

Social conditioning refers to the process by which individuals are influenced by social norms and values that shape their attitudes, beliefs, and behaviors. It is a powerful force that shapes our thoughts and actions, often without us even realizing it. Social conditioning is learned from a young age through family, peers, media, and other social institutions, and it can have a deep impact on how we perceive ourselves and others.

Of course, the leadership of women is encouraged but social conditioning can be detrimental to women assuming leadership roles because "from a young age, girls are often socialized to be caretakers and nurturers, while boys are encouraged to be leaders and assertive." Women tend to "undervalue and diminish" their professional skills, often having been "socialized to be more passive and deferential." Women are urged to break free from their conditioning through "education and mentorship" and challenge "stereotypes and biases," but these actions take asserting themselves, which may not be easy for women who have experienced years of conditioning that undermined their self-esteem. It is refreshing to note that encouraging women's leadership is a topic of conversation in business organizations, but the real task is to bolster girls' confidence in themselves from the beginning. This may be a job that feels like lifting yourself up by your own bootstraps, but breaking free of the gravity (pun intended) of low self-esteem may be the ticket to soar! As I frequently say, "You go girl!"

Sadhguru, an Eastern Indian yoga master, says, "The best thing you can do for your family, your children, society and the world around you is enhance yourself."

ARCHETYPES:
THE GODDESSES

Archetypes are models. The ageless prototypes portrayed in art, sculpture, rites, myths, and fairy tales were inspired by artists who did not study psychology. Awakening to the meaning of an archetype releases power in our psyches/souls and enhances our ability to see the world as it might have been experienced by the artists who created the original works of art. The potential of becoming conscious and truly sensing the meaning of an archetype connects us to the collective consciousness of all who perceive these images as representative of who we are ~ Spiritual Beings having Earthly experiences.

Today we are most familiar with archetypes through the work of psychologist Carl Jung. Tricia McCannon explains in *Return of the Divine Sophia*:

In Jungian thought, when we connect with a god or goddess we gain the power to draw on these qualities within ourselves. One aspect of the deity might symbolize courage, while another brings wisdom. One archetype might awaken a passion for music, while another inspires the pursuit of scientific understanding. In this way we call on many different archetypes within our own psyche to help balance our lives.

Perhaps it is wise to define what a Goddess is. Jalaja Bonheim, editor of *Goddess: A Celebration in Art and Literature*, says Goddesses are deities who reflect our own nature. She states:

> A dictionary defines a goddess as "a female being of supernatural powers or attributes." But many cultures do not conceive of matter and spirit as separate, nor do they distinguish between "natural" and "supernatural" phenomena. Read the stories of indigenous tribes, and you will soon realize that to them, everything, from the flight patterns of birds to the cycles of the moon, is miraculous, sacred, and suffused with spiritual presence. In their world, nothing is "supernatural," least of all a goddess, who represents the very essence of natural power. They perceive spirit as a stream that flows through all things, uniting plants, animals, humans, and spirits.

Starhawk, Baker and Hill, authors of *Circle Round: Raising Children in Goddess Traditions*, tell us that:

> The earliest Goddess cultures left no written records of their beliefs and rituals. The stories that have come down to us have been changed and altered with time. Much of the wisdom and values of the earliest Goddess traditions are still preserved in faery tales and folktales, but they are coated with the values and beliefs of the patriarchal cultures that followed. So to look at traditional tales requires us to decode them, to extract the symbols that are meaningful and transform the rest.

Merlin Stone wrote *When God Was a Woman* revealing "a past that has been buried by millennia of Judeo-Christian myth and corresponding social order." In our past the Goddess "was revered as the wise creator and the one source of universal order, not simply as a fertility symbol as some histories would have us believe."

In Goddess cultures "women bought and sold property, traded in the marketplace, and inherited title and land from their mothers."

It is wise to recognize that societies have reinterpreted original meanings of the Goddess to suit the dictates of those that prevail, typically the patriarchal institutions that have dominated cultures for aeons. There has been a great effort to eradicate the Goddess herself and to diminish feminine qualities within every woman considering them as lesser, unworthy, contemptible and valueless.

Elinor Gadon tells us in *The Once and Future Goddess,*

> Goddess religion was earth-centered, not heaven-centered, of this world not other-worldly, body-affirming not body-denying, holistic not dualistic. The Goddess was immanent, within every human being, not transcendent, and humanity was viewed as part of nature. . . . In our own time, in our own culture, the Goddess once again is becoming a symbol of empowerment for women, a catalyst for an emerging spirituality that is earth-centered; a metaphor for the earth as a living organism; an archetype for feminine consciousness; a mentor for healers; the emblem of a new political movement; an inspiration for artists; and a model for resacralizing woman's body.

Faith in the Divine Feminine has endured from time immemorial even though attempts have been made to eradicate her. Her images speak to our deeper minds giving our intuition and imaginations a chance to envision the possibilities of a Goddess to be courageous, to be a model of love, purity, beauty, joy, peace or truth. In spite of patriarchal attitudes, humanity has been worshipping Goddesses for aeons, holding these Divine Beings up as ideals to emulate.

Through images, archetypes, myths and stories both ancient and modern, this book views girls ~ women ~ through a lens that has been clouded for centuries but is clearing to reveal the Divine

Feminine as a radiant Being ready to express her Self. A few fairytales and myths are mentioned here for their inherent value in presenting and clarifying archetypes, while Goddesses portrayed in statuary and images on canvas and stone are center stage. The Goddesses that are included here exhibit qualities that we admire. We would like to be like them. *The Truth is, we are already!* Within us we have their virtues, even if we doubt ourselves.

Statues, paintings and hieroglyphs can remind us of who we are at the core of our Being. Many of the stories, legends and myths that abound are based in oral traditions that can be challenging to interpret, so the focus here is to view images that utilize our imaginations in visualizing the best in each woman. The images suggest metaphors that can reach beyond subconscious minds into the superconscious minds of the viewers to awaken them to the Beauty and Truth of who *they* are. We must sift through any illusions to find the gems of our Wholeness, our Holiness. What follows are qualities ~ the jewels ~ that are exemplified by Goddesses celebrated within various cultures throughout the ages.

The Spiral Dance: A Rebirth of the Ancient Religion of the Great Goddess by Starhawk emphasizes the importance of the Goddess for women today:

> The importance of the Goddess symbol for women cannot be overstressed. The image of the Goddess inspires women to see ourselves as divine, our bodies as sacred, the changing phases of our lives as holy, our aggression as healthy, our anger as purifying, and our power to nurture and create sustains all life . . . . Through the Goddess, we can discover our strength, enlighten our minds, own our bodies, and celebrate our emotions. We can move beyond narrow, constricting roles and become whole.

Marianne Williamson, inspiring author of *A Woman's Worth*, suggests:

Embrace the Goddess and her divine perception of you. Ask her to reveal to you the you she has in mind. Ask her to send you the relationships and circumstances that will foster that strength within you, that the world might be blessed by the presence of a woman in all her glory.

PALLAS ATHENA:
TRUTH, POWER & PROTECTION

We begin with Athena, who was revered as Pallas Athena in ancient Greece. She was known as the protectress of the city of Athens. The Parthenon, a temple built on the Acropolis, was dedicated to Athena. Many of her statues portray her with sword and shield, ready for battle. However, she is regarded as wise, a brilliant strategist who would rather use her wits to solve disagreements than resort to violence. Athena is thought of as virginal; she exemplifies independence, strength, courage and a profound sense of Self. Therefore, she is our first Goddess to demonstrate the value of Self-esteem.

Perhaps, most of all, Athena is known as the Goddess of Truth. Her message is one that is particularly important for us to know since we, as human beings with well-established egos, rationalize many of our thoughts, feelings and actions. We tell ourselves *rational-lies*. We need to reprogram our old beliefs and discern the greater Truth rather than a lie that breeds separation and duality. Athena reminds us that as we *know* the Truth, the Truth will set us free.

Pallas Athena has attributes that by today's standards may seem masculine, those attributed to the left brain. She exhibits power and authority, typically manly traits, as well as intellectual and strategic planning abilities. Nonetheless, she is also patron of the arts, weaving and handicrafts, more feminine endeavors in patriarchal society. She represents a balance of masculine and feminine qualities.

Images of Athena appear in countries around the world. The photograph here is the statue atop a magnificent marble fountain standing in front of the Austrian Parliament Building in Vienna. She holds in her right hand Nike, the Goddess of Victory. She suggests that Victory over adversity is possible, even a forgone conclusion, when we speak our Truth and demonstrate our Power.

A 42-foot statue of Athena stands in a full-size replica of the Parthenon in Nashville, Tennessee. In 2002 the statue was gilded with gold. She represents the glory of the Divine Feminine to those who can appreciate her visage.

Athena even appears in the rotunda of the United States Capitol building. Painted by Italian artist Constantino Brumidi in 1865 on the interior surface of the Capitol dome, this depiction of George Washington is known as the *Apotheosis of Washington*. It portrays the first president of the United States of America ascending into the Heavens flanked by the Goddesses of Liberty and Victory. These figures are surrounded by other Gods and Goddesses, angelic figures and symbolic representations of American ideals. Athena, also known also as the Roman Goddess Minerva, appears with inventors Robert Fulton, Benjamin Franklin and Samuel Morse. She signifies wisdom and inspiration for the invention of a printing press and an electric generator that depict innovations created in a free democratic society. Athena is among six Gods and Goddesses who are archetypes for the qualities embraced by the people of the United States of America.

Pallas Athena inspires us to acknowledge our power as creators, as potent women who can call upon our inner wisdom to have faith in ourselves and to overcome hardship. As Indian spiritual leader Sadhguru notes, "The roots of the Divine are entrenched in this body. If you nurture the roots, how can you avoid the flowering."

SOPHIA: WISDOM & ENLIGHTMENT

The wisdom of Athena leads naturally to Sophia, perhaps the most well-known Goddess of Wisdom. Across time and cultures, wisdom is highly regarded. The statue pictured here stands in Sofia, Bulgaria, a city named for this Goddess. She has an owl on her shoulder, symbolizing Divine Wisdom, and a laurel wreath in her right hand, signifying peace that accompanies the use of Wisdom instead of warfare. She is embossed with gold emphasizing her intrinsic value as a priceless quality of God.

The Hagia Sophia Grand Mosque in Istanbul, Turkey, is an architectural masterpiece. Built during the Byzantine Empire it was called the *Church of Holy Wisdom.* Originally a Greek Ortho-dox church, it became a mosque under the Ottoman Turks, was converted to a museum and, since 2020, is again a mosque. Today it bears the name Hagia Sophia, which means Holy Wisdom.

The Goddess Sophia is the personification of Wisdom. Under-standing, Enlightenment and Wisdom are feminine qualities asso-ciated with intuition, faculties of the right brain. Unfortunately, the dominance of patriarchal attitudes have for centuries valued left-brain thinking ~ reason, intelligence, language, analysis, logic ~ regarded as masculine and more valuable than intuition, creativ-ity and emotion.

In the book of Proverbs in the Old Testament (KJV), Wisdom speaks: "The Lord possessed me in the beginning of his way, before his works of old. I was set up from everlasting, from the beginning, or ever the earth was" (Proverbs 8:22-23). This personalization sug-gests that a feminine aspect of the Divine was an integral part of Creation. Before the existence of Earth, the balance of masculine and feminine, Father *and* Mother God, existed. In the third chapter of Proverbs Wisdom is praised: "She *is* more precious than rubies; and all the things thou canst desire are not to be compared unto her" (Proverbs 3:15). Devotees are advised by Father God to "get wisdom, get understanding: forget *it* not; neither decline from the words of my mouth. Forsake her not, and she shall preserve thee: love her, and she shall keep thee (Proverbs 4:5-6).

In the Scriptures Wisdom speaks as a person, and when spoken of is referred to as *She*, an indispensable value treasured by God. Thus, Wisdom is revered as an expression of the Divine Feminine, the companion of the Divine Masculine, and Cocreator of all that is. Some biblical scholars examining ancient Hebraic, Kabalistic, Christian, Gnostic and apocryphal texts interpret Wisdom as the equal of God. She is called Lady Wisdom and Dame Wisdom.

In *The New Book of Goddesses and Heroines* Patricia Monaghan conveys multiple images of Sophia:

> She is a fruit-bearing tree, she is a garment that shrouds and protects us, she is a working craftswoman of great skill, she is veiled, she is open. Full of contradiction and mystery, Sophia remained a potent symbol through many centuries and many countries, and continues to inspire the faithful of patriarchal regions today with a sense of feminine divinity.

Sophia reminds us of our Oneness, our connection to our Creative Source and to the Earth. In *Goddess: A Celebration in Art and Literature*, Sophia is described as multifaceted:

> For within her is a spirit intelligent, holy, unique, manifold, subtle, active, incisive, unsullied, lucid, invulnerable, benevolent, sharp, irresistible, beneficent, loving to man, steadfast, dependable, unperturbed, almighty, all-surveying, penetrating all intelligent, pure and most subtle spirits; for Wisdom is quicker to move than any motion; she is so pure, she pervades and permeates all things.

From ancient Scriptures we are told that regardless of culture, race, gender, or religion, we all have her glorious qualities within us. According to Caitlin Matthews in her book *Sophia: Goddess of Wisdom*:

> [Sophia] is primarily the keeper of earthly and heavenly wisdom and the guardian of its laws. . . . Sophia is gloriously beautiful, ageless, eternal, mediating, transcendent spirituality. . . . She is at hand as a living avatara of the Divine Feminine and for whom we yearn so urgently. . . . Open your heart, walk within and find Sophia.

Confucius said "By three methods we may learn wisdom: First, by reflection, which is noblest; second, by imitation, which is easiest; and third by experience, which is the bitterest." In the Far East, centuries ago, this philosopher known for his great wisdom shared this understanding: humanity can find wisdom by first going within.

Hildegard of Bingham, a German saint who lived in the 1100s, said, "I, the fiery life of *divine wisdom* (emphasis added), I ignite the beauty of the plains, I sparkle the water, I burn in the sun, and the moon, and the stars." Hildegard is known as a writer, composer, mystic, philosopher and an amazing visionary who literally identified with Divine Wisdom. Describing the work of Hildegard, scholar Rosemary Reuther says that:

> Wisdom is the means by which God brings all preexistent ideas to be manifest in material form. In this role, Wisdom can be spoken of as the Alpha and Omega, the beginning and the end of all things, who orders the whole creation.

It should be noted that the word *philosophy* literally means the love of wisdom, stemming from two Greek words, philia (love) and Sophia (wisdom). Wisdom is inherent in every human being. Each girl, each woman, indeed, each human being has an innate consciousness, an intuitive knowing. However, girls are not taught to regard their own inner wisdom and are taught to rely on external authorities, usually those deemed by patriarchal society to be more knowledgeable and trustworthy. Each girl, as she matures, should be respected for her wisdom which then reinforces her trust in her own truth.

THE VIRGIN OF GUADALUPE
MOTHER MARY:
LOVE & REVERENCE FOR ALL LIFE

There are few people who have not heard of the Blessed Virgin Mary. She is known by many names including Mother Mary, Queen of the Angels, Queen of Life, Gate of Heaven, Temple of the Living God, Mother of Eternal Glory and Our Lady. The magnificent cathedral in Paris is named for her ~ Notre Dame. This Cathedral caught fire several years ago and has been restored ~ resurrected ~ and celebrated so publicly that billions of people worldwide have been reawakened to *Our Lady*. The restoration of Notre Dame took five years to complete. It was reopened on December 8th, 2024, a day celebrated as an important Feast Day in the Latin Church. The day is known as the *Solemnity of the Immaculate Conception* which honors Mary as having been conceived without original sin.

The restored Notre Dame is reported to be a glorious unification of modern technology and medieval architecture. Stained glass windows now glow with special lighting which enhances the crystalline colors of figures and designs that have illuminated visitors for hundreds of years.

There have been reports of Mary's visitations over centuries, the most famous of which have been in Guadalupe, Mexico; Fatima, Portugal; Lourdes, France; and Medjugorje, Bosnia-Herzegovina. She has reportedly appeared to uneducated, young and trusting souls who are devout in their faith rather than scholars or skeptics.

In Mexico her image (shown here) is emblazoned on fabric, the tilma or cloak worn by Juan Diego, and preserved in a cathedral dedicated to Mary. In 1531 the Virgin Mary appeared to Juan Diego, an Aztec peasant. Ultimately her apparition was recognized by the Catholic church, and the Basilica of Our Lady of Guadalupe was erected in Villa de Guadalupe Hidalgo, now a northern section of Mexico City. Mary became the *Goddess of the Americas* as her cathedral stood counter to Spain's efforts to repress all the gods and goddesses of the indigenous people of South America in favor of God the Father and His Son. In *Goddesses and the Divine Feminine*, Rosemary Radford Ruether points out "the most extensive effort of patriarchal Christianity to repress all female symbols of the divine." Although some individuals doubt the apparitions, many believe in them so strongly that all the locations where Mary has been said to appear are littered with crutches, wheel chairs, braces and other signs of miraculous healings that have taken place at these sacred sites.

Joseph Campbell, renowned author of *Goddesses: Mysteries of the Feminine Divine,* suggests that, as the Virgin Mother of God, Mary is linked to the Goddess traditions. The Virgin of Guadalupe is included in *Goddesses: A World of Myth and Magic* by Burleigh Muten. In the picture of the Virgin here, as in many statues of Mary, she is standing on the crescent moon. This representation associates Mary with the cycles of the moon, "the changing lunar aspects of the Goddess," according to Tricia McCannon. To call Mary a Goddess certainly seems appropriate.

Devotees have loved and revered Mary for over two thousand years. She is the embodiment of Love, the Divine Comforter. In the New Testament she is the mother of Jesus. Mary is described as a virgin who was told by Archangel Gabriel that she would bear the Son of God whom she would name Jesus (Luke 1:26-38); thus, she represents both virginity *and* motherhood, a paradox capable of being achieved by a Goddess. Marguerite Rigoglioso has written a book on this subject: *Virgin Mother Goddesses of Antiquity*. She explains "that nearly all such pre-Greek goddesses were understood to be both generative mothers and virgins simultaneously."

Prayers and songs to Mary are conveyed in many languages and often begin with "Ave Maria" or "Hail Mary." She is thought to be unconditionally loving, neither judgmental nor critical. It is interesting that little is said of her in the New Testament, but during the establishment of early Christianity the founders recognized the love of the ancient Goddess among those they sought to convert to the new religion, and subsequently Mary was embraced as the feminine face of the Divine.

The return of the Divine Feminine is recognized throughout the world as the long-awaited restoration of the balance of the masculine and feminine aspects of God. The Holy Trinity is redefined to clarify its meaning. Considered throughout the centuries within old patriarchal beliefs as The Father, Son and Holy Spirit, all of which were construed to be male, the new (and perhaps original) interpretation is that the Trinity represents the union of Father God, Mother God ~ the Holy Spirit ~ and the product of their union, the Sons and Daughters of God. This concept embraces the Feminine aspect of God and the half of the world's population that has been considered less than, unworthy and the cause of the downfall of humanity because Eve tempted Adam with the proverbial fruit. Many world religions have glorified a single male, punitive God while disparaging women and denying that all Children of God are the result of the union of the Divine Masculine *and* Divine Feminine aspects of God. No child is born without a Mother.

It is Mary who has worn the mantle of the Divine Feminine in both Eastern and Western traditions for two millennia. She is esteemed by her devotees for her support, guidance, and uplifting Presence. Her Love is valued for the maternal protection believers feel she provides. She is thought by some to have been born without original sin and upon her death ascended into Heaven. Prayers to Mary invoke the purity of her love to bring about miracles.

WHITE TARA: THE CORE OF PURITY WITHIN

White Tara has been worshipped for centuries and is still revered today. "To this day," remarks the editor of *Goddess: A Celebration in Art and Literature*, "the Tibetan people worship the goddess Tara as the eternal mother who gives their lives 'a foundation like the earth.'" This Goddess, honored in both Hindu and Buddhist religions, soothes and calms her devotees. She is among a number of Taras including Green, Red, Blue, and Yellow Tara. Each has unique Divine Feminine qualities.

White Tara symbolizes goodness and purity as well as Peace and Unity. She is reputed to have reached enlightenment and could have ascended to Nirvana but chose to remain close to the Earth as a Bodhisattva, one who is spiritually awake but chooses to serve all beings until they awaken as well, in service to all humanity. She eliminates obstacles on humanity's path to spiritual freedom and enlightenment.

Renee Starr recounts a vision experienced by the Buddha in *You Are Woman, You Are Divine: The Modern Woman's Journey Back to the Goddess*. The Buddha sees that White Tara, the sister of Green Tara:

> Was as motionless as a tree. Her skirt was as white as the whitest cloud in the sky above her head. She moved with the grace and ease of a snowflake, light and airy as it floated down to the earth. White Tara expressed all the calm and silence of life, being the embodiment of the in-between times. She was the very moment just before an intake of breath, and the moment just after the exhale. She was the quiet of the dawn just before the sun rose up over the horizon, and the awe of the instant before dusk when the sun dipped low and disap-

peared beneath the sky. She was the moment in time just before life began, as well as the second before it ended.

White Tara's energy is pacifying. Images of her like the one pictured here appear on thangkas, paintings usually framed with beautiful brocade and seen hanging on walls in homes and temples. She is seated meditating with her legs crossed in a yogic lotus position and resting on a lotus blossom. She has seven eyes: in addition to the two we all have, Tara has an eye in the middle of her forehead, known as the third eye, which gives her the ability to see ultimate reality ~ a bigger picture ~ beyond what mere mortals can perceive in physical reality. She has an eye in the palm of each hand, and one on the sole of each foot. These eyes represent her ability to sense Humanity's suffering while she remains peaceful and offers comfort to all those who ask for her help. She is surrounded by a halo of light, her aura radiating a rainbow of brilliant colors.

Tara is regal, the essence of an all-seeing, omnipresent, omnipotent and omniscient Goddess. Like Pallas Athena she is powerful and protective; like Sophia she is wise; like Mother Mary she is loving; and like Kuan Yin, whom we will meet soon, she is compassionate. She embodies the ideal of a female who attains enlightenment and is said to have vowed to return lifetime after lifetime in a female body to show that enlightenment was possible for women as well as men.

In Sanskrit, Tara means *star*. Perhaps our inclination to make a wish upon a star is derived from looking to the Heavens and asking for Divine intervention from this powerful Goddess. Tara has achieved self-mastery and is the essence of composure and serenity. Therefore, she is a Star Goddess to whom human beings pray to overcome their fears. To invoke her aid Devotees chant her mantra *Om tare tuttare ture Soha* 108 times counting repetitions on a mala often made of lotus seeds. This mantra is a prayer which is said to mean "I bow to the Mother of All those who have overcome the endless cycle of death and rebirth."

How alike many of our practices are even though we think our religions are so different. Reciting White Tara's manta connects us with her energy, the energy that is already, perhaps lying dormant, within us.

Goddesses remind us of qualities we have within. We seek to emulate the virtues of these Divine Archetypes. The real power to master our emotions, to have unlimited and enlightened minds, to overcome our fears, to be calm in the face of outer appearances, is within us. We simply have not been taught to look within. In fact, we have been taught to look to external sources for relief from discomfort. That relief can take the form of a rescuer, the proverbial knight in shining armor, or drugs, either prescription or recreational, substances such as alcohol or cigarettes, sensual or sexual experiences ~ the list is endless. None of these remedies is a function of our Higher Selves. They are the tools our egos employ to keep us stuck in old habit patterns so that through our senses we keep doing what we have always done. Our habitual choices, both conscious and unconscious, are familiar but do not let us improve the quality of our lives.

It is said that all of our problems, including those of ill health, stem from our own thoughts which focus our attention on what is wrong rather than what is right, that is, on good health or other positive qualities and how we desire our lives to be.

White Tara symbolizes restoration, renewal, resurrection and ascension into Higher Dimensions. She holds the immaculate concept for every motive and desire, pure and unadulterated by our lower human egos. We must hold the vision of our desires already accomplished and serving the Highest Good for all concerned. Beloved Tara, and all the Goddess energies, are examples of who we truly are and how we can be successful as we journey through our lives.

IXCHEL:
HEALING & INNER VISION

Ixchel, pronounced *ee shell*, is a Mayan Goddess of healing and childbirth. Her statue, shown here, is located at a resort in Punta Sur on Isla Mujeres ~ the island of women ~ Quintana Roo, off the Yucatan Peninsula of Mexico. Many Goddess images have been appropriated by commercial enterprises for advertising and the promotion of products and services because their positive imagery (archetypes) is carried in our collective unconscious minds, especially images of motherhood and Divine Feminine Wisdom.

Ixchel is a Goddess of the Moon, medicine and midwifery. She nurtures women through pregnancy and childbirth. She is called upon by women to conceive, to have healthy pregnancies and to give birth easily. Legends tell us of this Goddess, in her guise as a crone, that is, an elderly wise woman with extensive knowledge and experience, who gathers other midwives together to attend or preside over births. "She is still known as The Queen, Our Grandmother, Our Mother and The White Lady" according to Hallie Iglehart Austen in *The Heart of the Goddess: Art, Myth and Meditations of the World's Sacred Feminine.*

Ixchel is regarded as a Goddess of Fertility, but she serves throughout a woman's life cycle as a triple goddess representing a sensual young woman and the ability to procreate; motherhood, and the energies of productivity and reproductivity; and, the aged crone who assists those women younger than herself to make life transitions. As Goddess of the Moon she is attuned to Nature's rhythms and the earthly cycles of the tides as well as women's monthly cycles that enable them to bring forth new life. She is strongly associated with the water element and carries a jar from which water could pour. This is particularly relevant during the

Age of Aquarius, which has the zodiacal sign of the Water Bearer who pours water from the Heavens to nurture the Earth.

Ixchel is also a patroness of womanly crafts, particularly textile work and weaving. Together with the Sun God, she is said to be co-creator of the world, literally weaving the cosmos into existence. The myths and legends available today have been constructed by historians, archeologists, and those who collect oral histories and interpret the carvings and sculptures that remain to depict an entire culture. One myth relates that having been rejected by the Sun (the sun and the moon do not occupy the Heavens at the same time; the moon follows the Sun through the sky as night follows the day), Ixchel demonstrated her independence and Divine purpose to be in service to women as a healer and midwife.

This Ixchel is a Goddess of Procreation, including the sexual act of union between male and female. She helps women appreciate themselves by modeling independence and self-reliance while also being supported by other women in the physical process of childbearing. Her devotees would make pilgrimages to her shrines on the islands of Cozumel and Isla Mujeres to ensure happy and fruitful marriages. Legends tell of her encouraging women to engage in a sweatbath before and after giving birth. The jar that she carries may have been a receptacle for healing unguents or to hold the placenta which ancient cultures would plant near a tree in honor of the new life just born. Ixchel's jar is called a *Birth Vase*, suggesting its importance in childbearing. It reminds us of the alabaster jar that held precious oil with which Jesus was anointed. Perhaps anointing with oil is a tradition celebrating the beginning of life, even a new life resurrected from the old.

Images of Ixchel show her wearing an ornate headdress. It sometimes has weaving implements in it and always seems to have a snake emerging from the front of the headpiece. This is suggestive of the crowns worn by the Pharaohs of ancient Egypt. These snakes symbolize to metaphysicians the ascendance of Kundalini energies, the high spiritual nature of the Pharaoh. Snakes shed their skins and, therefore, symbolize transformation. Emerging from the forehead of the Goddess, the third eye is open and her inner vision is awake. This Goddess knows herself. She can focus, concentrate and even consecrate with her ability to heal and make another whole and holy. It is interesting that hieroglyphs and carvings of Gods and Goddesses in both the East and West contain this same imagery.

Other images show Ixchel holding a rabbit. Like the Chinese, the Mayans saw a rabbit when they looked at the face of the moon. What may be more to the point is that rabbits are famous for their fertility and prolific reproductive abilities. This would be a perfect totem for a Goddess who promoted pregnancy and childbearing.

The rabbit also signifies the Goddess's relationship to all life: animals, plants and minerals as well as humans. This imagery suggests coming into balance with our environment, demonstrating reverence for all life and respect for animals who can act as guides, familiars, and allies on life's path.

LADY VENUS:
DIVINE GRACE & BEAUTY

Lady Venus is the essence of Divine Grace and Beauty. In the painting by Botticelli called the *Birth of Venus* she arises from the ocean on a scallop shell. In Greek culture Venus is known as Aphrodite. She is said to have adopted the qualities of Aphrodite and, through her, was able to embody characteristics of other foreign goddesses from ages past. Venus is related to Astarte, an ancient Phoenician Goddess of beauty; to Mesopotamian Ishtar, Goddess of loving bonds between individuals, families and communities; and to Sumerian Goddess Inanna, the first Goddess for whom there is written evidence.

Venus is identified with the planet Venus, sister planet of Earth, which is sometimes called the morning or the evening star. This bright light in the sky is said to be a celestial form of the Goddess who guides believers on their life paths. *Venia*, a Roman word that correlates with Venus, was spoken to bring forth tangible evidence of the Goddess' favor.

Because Lady Venus is associated with love and feminine beauty, she has been favored as a subject of paintings, sculptures, mosaics and murals for millennia. Even today her name is used in movie titles and commercial advertising for products designed for women, everything from bathing suits to razor blades. Most known for her beauty, she is often pictured nude. This portrayal appears to link her with the misuse of this attribute. Myths describe her promiscuous behavior and she is considered a Goddess of prostitutes. It seems as though, like other great feminine figures of the past, she has been disparaged by patriarchal institutions including religions and governments. However, Julius Caesar claimed that Venus was his Divine ancestor and, in opposition to her portrayal as a patroness of harlots, she was regarded as a Goddess who could transform libidinous behavior into virtuous conduct.

Coming-of-age stories relate the surrender of the toys of their childhoods to Venus when girls reached puberty. Today some families celebrate the passage of a girl to womanhood with a quinceañera in Latin American cultures, or a bat mitzvah in Jewish cultures. Some secular families create their own ceremonies by giving their adolescents car keys!

Lady Venus blesses brides insuring happy, fruitful marriages. By consecrating the union of man and woman, Venus demonstrates Divine Grace and assures enduring connubial bliss. The Goddess honors the balance of masculine/feminine in the newlywed's partnership rather than endorsing a traditional patriarchal relationship in which masculine energy dominates the feminine.

Having been born full-grown from the sea, Venus is associated with water which represents emotional qualities, both tranquil and stormy. Symbols of Venus include sea shells, roses and myrtle, a plant thought to be an aphrodisiac ~ a word derived from Aphrodite - and used to adorn bridal crowns and bouquets. Cherubs often hover around images of Venus, signifying aspects of her name, since the Latin noun *venus* means love. The word *Venus* stems from the Latin verb *venerari*, which means *to revere*. This is devotion, worship of the Divine. The English word *venerate* is derived from this verb. In Hindu tradition Parvati demonstrates devotional worship. Like Venus she represents love and beauty and is still worshipped today.

Different forms of love are part of other cultures. For example, Greek filial love signifies deep friendship or family love; pragma is a mature and lasting love; eros or erotic love implies romantic, passionate love; storge is the bonding love we feel for our children; agape love is more universal love for humanity. Eros can be consuming and demanding while agape love is given freely and stems from one's honor of self.

Venus is frequently portrayed viewing herself in a mirror. This is thought to be vanity, an obsessive form of self-esteem. It is, however, a way to see one's worth, one's inner beauty no matter what the image. Margaret Starbird, author of *The Woman with the Alabaster Jar*, says the mirror of Venus:

Reflects the understanding that the material cosmos, embodied in the feminine (*matter* comes from Latin *mater*, meaning "mother"), is the mirror image of divinity and is understood to be the "other half" or counterpart of the spiritual. It is the physical world that manifests the unseen creative energy of the universe "in the flesh." In this sense, the material cosmos (feminine in the ancient cosmologies) "catches the spirit" in her mirror and holds it there, making it visible, as the ocean reflects the wholeness of the sky or the moon the light of the sun. Perhaps this explains why the love goddess is associated with a mirror. It is certainly not because she is vain; it is because she is the mirror image of the unseen positive energy of the cosmos.

A mirror's reflection returns to us what we share with the world. As an expression of the Law of Attraction, looking into a mirror can remind us to be accountable, to acknowledge that our impression in the outer world is reflected at every moment in the Mirror of Life. The circumstances we witness are the reflection of our own thoughts, words, feelings, and actions. It is wise to look through the eyes of the Goddess Venus to see the best in yourself and the results you generate.

Giving up ourselves, making ourselves small or less than to love another is never the right thing to do. The beauty of who we are must be honored as we give love from a place of wholeness. This Divine Love uplifts all who receive it, including the giver. Devotion to the Divine Feminine *and* Divine Masculine, both within and without, perfectly expresses the Divine Grace of Venus.

KUAN YIN:
MERCY, COMPASSION & FORGIVENESS

Kuan Yin, sometimes spelled Guanyin or Kwan Yin, is known worldwide as the Goddess of Mercy, Compassion and Forgiveness. In the book *Kuan Yin, Myths and Prophecies of the Chinese Goddess of Compassion:*

> Kuan Yin knows no religious boundaries. She graces virtually all Taoist temples and all sacred Mountains; she is found in almost all Chinese Buddhist temples; she is revered in Shintoism and even Christianity has an understanding of her and her significance.

Daniela Schenker notes in *Kuan Yin: Accessing the Power of the Divine Feminine* that altars in both East and West hold figurines of both Mother Mary and Kuan Yin.

She is worshipped today throughout the orient where statues are erected to her at sacred sites. The Kuan Yin of Nanshan is 354 feet tall and is located on the south coast of the Chinese island province of Hainan. She radiates her blessings and protection to devotees and the entire world. The Hainan figure has three features; one depicts Kuan Yin gesturing with her right hand while holding a sutra (a Buddhist scripture) in her left; one aspect has palms crossed while holding a mala, a string of prayer beads; and the third facet holds a lotus flower, a symbol of purity and the ability to rise above adversity. This enormous statue, pictured here, took six years to build and was enshrined in 2005 with 108 (the number of beads in a mala) Buddhist monks from mainland China, Macao, Hong Kong and Taiwan who participated in the ceremony among thousands of pilgrims.

Colossal statues of Kuan Yin have been built in Guandong and in Ningxiang, China. The Kuan Yin in Guandong is a seated figure 203 feet tall sitting on a pedestal 50 feet high. The Guishan Guanyin of the Thousand Eyes in Ningxiang is 325 feet tall and has many arms representing the Goddess' infinite abilities to serve humanity. A temple dedicated to Kuan Yin in Honolulu, Hawaii, features a huge golden statue of the Goddess. A YouTube presentation shows her followers offering fruit, flowers, and incense which they are placing on her altar.

Kuan Yin has been worshipped for centuries. Her origins seem to arise from ancient India and had a male form as Avalokiteshvara. This expression of the Divine Masculine was committed to liberating all human beings from suffering. When the Heart Sutra (a sacred Buddhist text) was introduced in China, his attributes were considered more feminine and, through translations into Chinese, a feminine form of the Divine, the Goddess Kuan Yin, arose. She is still revered as an expression of the Divine Feminine around the world and is the most popular Chinese deity. She is believed to be so powerful that she can assist a devotee to overcome the need to reincarnate which keeps human beings trapped in the endless cycle of rebirth working out their karma.

In the West karma is known as the Law of Cause and Effect. In Christianity it is referred to as reaping what we sow. Judaic scriptures note only that retribution is achieved by an eye for an eye, which is an incomplete picture since friendly acts like hugs and kisses also rebound. In quantum physics this concept is discussed as magnetization and radiation and Like Attracts Like. Young people today often say "What goes around comes around." It is important to know that energy responds to this Law of Attraction. This knowledge helps us become accountable for our thoughts, words, feelings and actions because what we send out will return to us magnified as it picks up like energy on its way back.

Kuan Yin is likened to the Virgin Mary. In fact some statues and paintings of Kuan Yin have been specifically designed to combine the images from the Buddhist and Christian traditions to heal the disparity between the two faiths. A statue of Kuan Yin in Seoul, Korea was fashioned by a Catholic sculptor who deliberately incorporated the image of Mother Mary with the intention of reconciling differences between religions in Korean society. Images of Kuan Yin holding a baby evoke feelings of love and compassion much as images of Mother Mary holding baby Jesus do. Kuan Yin, like Mother Mary, is considered the patron saint of mothers and her images grace medical facilities in Taiwan to bless patients of all religions. In both Korea and Japan she is known as Kannon.

Compassion for family matters appeal to many of her followers, most of whom are women. She is known as the Goddess of Divine Family Life. Her popularity in the Orient seems due to the perception that Kuan Yin has infinite compassion for humanity as well as for the notion that she works in and through her devotees. She does not dominate or dictate. She is a companion who works *with* each individual bringing out the best from within them.

Poems attributed to Kuan Yin have been translated into English. One called *It's You* states:

There's a treasury full of jade and jewels: it is in you. Don't go searching far from home for it—it's here.

Kuan Yin promotes forgiveness. She encourages us to *let go* of the past, particularly those limiting beliefs and thoughts that create havoc in our present-day lives. One definition of forgiveness is *letting go of the idea that you could have had a different or better past*. When we obsess about our past it is like bringing yesterday's garbage into our home today. By not accepting what is, we are doomed to disappointment. Prayers to Kuan Yin can invoke her

Presence to lift the pall of discord and discontent to free us, to help us accept what we cannot change. In the well-known Serenity Prayer, we ask for acceptance of those things we can't change, the courage to change what we can, and the wisdom to know the difference. Those who invoke the Love and acceptance of Kuan Yin, the courage and Truth of Pallas Athena, or the Wisdom of Sophia are asking for serenity and peace of mind. As archetypes of the Divine Feminine, the Goddesses are present in many of our invocations, concealed inside the very qualities we seek. What Kuan Yin and each Goddess would tell us is that those virtues are already ours.

AMATERASU:
CLARITY, DIVINE PERCEPTION & DISCERNMENT

Amaterasu is the Goddess of the Sun, the central deity of Japanese religion and mythology. The Japanese royal family traces its lineage back to this Goddess. She is a significant deity in the Shinto religion and is honored at both private and public shrines. The most sacred shrine in Japan, the Grand Shrine of Ise, is frequented by worshipers who make pilgrimages there. This temple is rebuilt every twenty years to ensure that it will exist eternally. Ceremonies conducted by priests of Amaterasu at the Ise Shrine include prayers for Japan's royal family, for world peace, and for an abundant fall harvest. The Japanese flag displays a red disc on a white background which symbolizes the sun's illumination in the purity of Heaven. Japan is known as *The Land of the Rising Sun.*

As the Sun rises devotees bow to this ancient Goddess each morning. Amaterasu is called the *Spirit Shining in Heaven.* She is the Creatrix, creating each new day with her glorious Light. Amaterasu's name in Japanese is Amaterasu-omikami which translates as *the great kami* (goddess) *who shines in the sky* or the *Great Divinity Illuminating Heaven.*

Myths tell us that this powerful Goddess became enraged at her brother's disgusting and abusive behavior. When a beloved weaver woman died of wounds received from an act committed by Amaterasu's violent brother, the Goddess retreated to a cave and refused to come out. Without the Sun, crops withered and life on Earth began to die. Other Gods and Goddesses attempted to woo Amaterasu out of the cave, but to no avail. In a great gathering, these Divine Beings decided to place a mirror at the entrance to the cave. Their noisy dancing and laughter aroused Amaterasu's curiosity. She rolled back the stone guarding the cave entrance and peeked out. Seeing her beauty and radiance reflected in the mirror, she recognized her own Light that was needed by a dark and dying world. She came forth from the cave to again share her dazzling Light and continues to do so every day.

Within the metaphor we see that each of us must share our Light to fully illuminate the world. With our expanded awareness we see that violence, particularly abuse directed toward women, must end. Allowing our Divine Feminine qualities to be expressed is essential for the health of humanity and the Earth. Feminine virtues are honoring ourselves, speaking our truth, knowing that we are worthy of respect and love. We can see ourselves clearly, perceiving our inherent Light, and discern the value of letting our Light shine for ourselves and for others.

As the Goddess of the Sun, Amaterasu's greatest gift was to bring Light to the world. When she hid herself in a cave, the world was plunged into darkness. The message for us is clear. Indeed, clarity, discernment and Divine perception are traits of Beloved Amaterasu. When she yielded to her negative emotions, her vision was clouded. She succumbed to the illusion that circumstances were so bad that she had to hide rather than shine her Light. This seems to be what we often do in the face of misfortune. Just the opposite is true. This is when our Light is needed most. Our emotions may seem overpowering, but they can be controlled and even transcended.

When we focus on our Light, who we are at the core of our Being, we can perceive a bigger picture. We may be able to see facets of a situation that we had missed, or a broader view that considers the thoughts and feelings of others which we may have overlooked. We have the potential of shifting the behavior of others by holding a higher vision instead of focusing on their negativity. This is a noble idea and may be counterintuitive at first. Never do we put ourselves in harm's way to attempt to change another. We can, however, move beyond victim consciousness to esteem ourselves. This is the essence of Self-Esteem which Amaterasu realized and modeled by shining her Light.

THEMIS:
HARMONY, BALANCE, CONFIDENCE & ASSURANCE

The qualities of harmony and balance are exemplified by the Goddess Themis, the personification of Divine Justice. She is often portrayed carrying the scales of justice and is blindfolded as justice is impartial and should not be biased by preconceived ideas or prejudices.

Standing in front of the United States Supreme Court Building is a large seated statue of Contemplation. In her right hand she holds a smaller figure of the Goddess of Divine Justice, Themis, who is blindfolded and carrying her scales. With her eyes covered this Goddess listens carefully and makes decisions based on unbiased consideration of the facts. She is balanced within, using both her masculine ability to analyze data and her feminine intuition. She suggests that "As above, so below, as within, so without, as the universe, so the soul…." This quote is attributed to Hermes Trismegistus, a legendary figure who embodied the Greek God Hermes and the Egyptian God Thoth. It means that Heaven (above) and Earth (below) are One. What we think and feel inside (within) is also expressed in the outer world (without). It tells us that the Universe and the Soul (the essence of our Being) are the same. Spiritual traditions and quantum physics tell us this as well. We are One.

This Goddess of Balance represents not only the internal balance of wise decision-making, but an internal *and* external balance of our Masculine and Feminine qualities. When we use both our right and left brains, when we apply logic *and* creativity to problems we face, we feel confident and self-assured. We know that we are balanced, in harmony, calling upon the best of our natures to derive optimum solutions to issues we face, and we feel more in harmony with the world.

Themis is able to weigh events from the past, the present and the future applying her inner vision. She is said to have built the Oracle of Delphi and was able to predict events as an oracle herself. This is sometimes attributed to one's ability to access information through the Third Eye, an energy center between the brows. Focus at this location can enhance both inner and outer awareness. Each energy center is called a chakra (which means *wheel* in Sanskrit) in the Eastern Indian yogic tradition and each chakra should be balanced as well. Classes in yoga, breathwork, meditation, mindfulness and other energy modalities can acquaint us with ways to balance and harmonize our chakras and our physical, mental, emotional and etheric bodies.

When Gods and Goddesses were worshipped, devotees sometimes thought that they did not have the qualities embodied by each of the deities. Idols were revered that represented positive virtues but those merits were not considered to be components of the devotees themselves. Today we are recognizing that God/Goddess-qualities are actually inherent within each of us. We have been told we are children of the Creative Source and, therefore, are Reflections of the Divine. This recognition is both a blessing and a responsibility. As Themis exemplifies fairness and Divine Justice, she also awakens us to the idea that we are all subject to Universal Law.

The Law of Gravity is such a Law. We know that if we jump off a roof we will fall to the ground. It is unavoidable, as this is a law of physics on planet Earth. Other Laws have been revealed to us in spiritual philosophies and scriptures for millennia. Since the results of these Laws are harder to see or take time to manifest, we tend to overlook them. One of these Laws is known by different names including The Law of Cause and Effect, the Law of Attraction, and the Law of the Circle.

The portion of this book discussing Kuan Yin introduced this concept, but it is worth amplifying here. Every thought and feeling is energetic and what you are thinking and feeling is energetically expressed in the Universe. It is essential for anyone who is seeking Self-Realization, Self-Actualization, enhanced Self-Esteem or simply inner peace and harmony to know this eternal truth: we reap what we sow; we experience the return of our thoughts, feelings, words, and deeds. It can be an overwhelming idea to realize that every thought we think or emotion we feel is being sent out into the world ~ that they are creative and they come back! It begins to make sense that if we want happy lives, it behooves us to send out positive energy.

Picture thoughts and feelings as if they were sound waves. When speaking words unseen waves of energy travel from your mouth to the ears of those who hear you. Those sound waves are converted within the ears of your listener into impulses transmitted on circuits within their brains to be comprehended. What an amazing process.

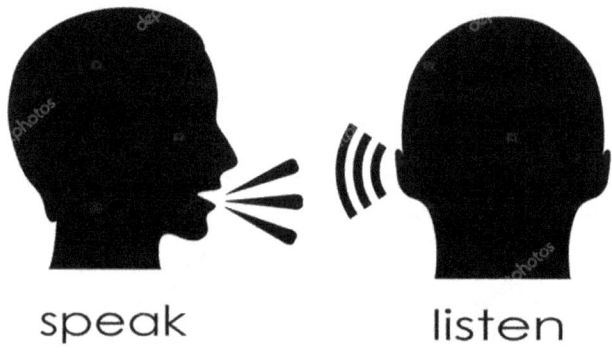

speak   listen

Or you can think of this process as sending a letter to someone: they get the message and send it back to you with a like-kind but more intense response. The way this shows up in our lives is in the results we experience. For example, if we send out loving thoughts and appreciation we might get an unexpected check in the mail. If we send out hateful thoughts to someone we might trip and fall, or have a car accident.

We receive reflections of thoughts and feelings that we never voice. They arise from our subconscious minds, our implicit memories, but they still have energy that will be projected from us and ultimately returned to us. These can come from beliefs that were imprinted before we were consciously aware of what was going into our memory banks. You might say to yourself, "I don't trust anyone. I'm always disappointed. Things don't work for me." And, in no time at all, you get to be right! Someone lies to you; your relationship fails; you lose your job. We think these things are unrelated. We call them coincidences, but they are the results of our own thoughts and feelings! What a responsibility!

Themis has been holding her scales up for centuries. We can now see them and what they represent with new eyes. In classical Greek mythology Themis is interested in Divine Law and Order, not human laws. Although we see her statue in cities like Frankfurt, Germany (pictured here), we do not hear the mythology associated with her. Themis also carries a sword, which represents her extraordinary power. She is not to be disregarded, as that invokes another deity, the Goddess Nemesis. The inevitable return of what we put out ~ that is, our thoughts and feelings ~ is governed by this deity. The word *nemesis* is still in our vocabulary today. It means an adversary we have difficulty overcoming. Ancient worshippers acknowledged returning energies, and probably asked for relief from the inevitable consequences of their actions. We can avoid negative consequences by sending out only what we would like to get back, although that takes effort and practice as our lives reflect back to us many things we did not even know we were catalyzing. This principle, known as the Golden Rule, has been encoded in every religion: do unto others what you would have them do unto you.

Before we leave the topic of balance it is worth mentioning Maat, the Egyptian Goddess of Justice, Harmony and Balance. Maat maintained the order and balance of the Universe itself.

In a ceremony she determined the worthiness of those departing this world to enter paradise. On her scales Maat would weigh the heart/soul of each deceased person against a feather. No wonder we value being light-hearted!

PAX & LAKSHMI:
PEACE & PROSPERITY FOR ALL

Peace ~ the Latin word is *Pax* ~ is pictured here in a beautiful carved marble bas-relief. It is from an altar in Rome called the *Ara Pacis Auguste* and is dedicated to peace. This type of sculpture is seen on a wall in which the chosen images stand out from the background which is cut away. In this stunning image Pax/Peace is personified as a mother holding two children. It suggests the Goddess Gaia, Mother Earth, as Earth is represented by abundant vegetation, while air is represented by the swan taking flight and water by the sea creature. Both the female figures on the right and left have billowing veils signifying wind, the air element. The outside figures are relaxed and domesticated animals rest at the Goddess' feet.

A Greek Goddess of Peace is Eirene, and she is also the Goddess of Spring. It is during peaceful times that crops can be raised, animals herded and trade/commerce can contribute to the prosperity of all. Abundance flows when peace prevails.

Peace and prosperity are two sides of the same coin. One is not truly possible without the other. If there is great disparity between those who have abundance and those who experience lack ~ the haves and the have nots ~ there is always dissention. If Peace does not exist, it seems that humanity cannot enjoy the abundance of this Earth. War ravages the Earth and destroys crops, buildings and life in all forms. Both of these bounties, peace and prosperity, need to be considered at the same time. Indian guru Sadhguru says "Peace is not the highest good in life. It is the most fundamental requirement."

Prosperity is represented in Hindu traditions by Lakshmi, Goddess of Wealth. Here she is seated on a lotus blossom, a symbol of purity and beauty. She has four arms which symbolize: "*dharma* (pursuit of ethical, moral life), *artha* (pursuit of wealth, means of life), *kama* (pursuit of love, emotional fulfillment), and *moksha* (pursuit of self-knowledge, liberation)." Lakshmi is often portrayed with elephants which represent strength. When accompanied by Ganesha, the powerful elephant-headed God, all obstacles to abundance are removed.

Lakshmi carries a lotus blossom in one or both hands symbolizing self-realization. Lotuses grow in water, rather dirty, so the metaphor suggests that regardless of our circumstances, we can rise above them; our purity remains intact and we can achieve higher states of consciousness. Lakshmi is known as the *Lotus Goddess* and is thought to have floated on a lotus before time and the world were created.

Lakshmi is adorned with gold and, as in this picture, holds a jar that contains great wealth. Golden coins fall from her jar. Her complement is the God Vishnu who upholds peace and justice so that abundance can be experienced. This balance of the masculine and feminine aspects of the Divine are essential to the flow of both peace and prosperity.

As we come into the realization that prosperity is our Divine Birthright and *wanting* sabotages the manifestation of our desires, we can begin to change the language we use when we think of abundance. We think we *want* to be prosperous but this language is truly self-defeating. *Wanting* is not having. Our brain/mind is so literal. When we want something, our mind assumes the goal is the act of *wanting*. Therefore, like the donkey who endlessly follows a carrot on the stick suspended in front of it, we strive for whatever it is that we *want*, but will never actually attain. Our mind focuses our attention on the *wanting* instead of the achievement. This thinking keeps the goal just out of our reach.

Our thoughts must be the result of our belief in ourselves, that we are truly worthy and deserving of prosperity. When we *know* we are made in the Goddess' image, possessing all her

Divine qualities, *wanting* transforms into having, into tangible results and the realization of our desires.

We can affirm our goals by visualizing them already accomplished, using our thoughts and words to bring them about instead of sabotaging our own success. The well-known 23rd Psalm, an Old Testament poem known to both Christians and Jews, states: "The Lord is my shepherd; I shall *not* want." This is a mandate! When we know we are God's children, we have no need to *want*. We simply ask the Divine for our heart's desire and see it in our inner vision manifested in reality. Over time our vision becomes our reality. Asking with clarity and intention, we receive. Our job is to ask, receive and appreciate.

FREYA:
JOY, ENTHUSIASM & DIVINE PURPOSE

Like the interconnectedness of Peace and Prosperity, Joy is inextricably linked to our Purpose in life. When we are doing what we love to do, we are enthused and happy. When we don't know what our Purpose is, we can perform a job that provides a paycheck, but we may not feel any real satisfaction. Knowing our

Purpose arises from within ourselves as we grow in understanding and wisdom. We begin to see how each of the Divine qualities represented by the Goddesses weave into one another. We see that Divine Wisdom and Inner Vision illuminate our knowledge of ourselves and, thus, we realize what gifts we bring to share with the world.

All Goddesses are personifications of joy and appreciation for life. Each knows her own Truth and how she can best serve humanity. Freya (sometimes spelled Freyja) is a Nordic Goddess whose statue stands in Stockholm, Sweden. In the illustration here she is driving a chariot pulled by two cats. Certainly a lady (Freya means *lady*) who can control cats that are renowned for their independence is on purpose in her life. Sometimes things that are hard to organize or accomplish are referred to as being as difficult to do as herding cats! Freya handles this task with ease.

Freya is considered the most beautiful of the Goddesses and the most sensuous. She is the Goddess of love and fertility. She is believed to care for pregnant women and those giving birth. Stories tell of her riding in her chariot, hovering over battles so that she can lift the spirits of slain soldiers to her celestial mansion and they can reside in Valhalla (paradise) for eternity. Thus, she assists human beings at birth *and* death.

Plants like Freya's Hair are named for this lovely Goddess. The day of the week, Friday, is named for her. This is the last workday of the week, the day that we begin to celebrate before we return to our jobs when the workweek commences on Monday. Freya's tears turn to gold, thus the golden mineral amber is called Freya's Tears. The Danish national anthem contains a phrase calling the country "Freya's Hall."

Other Goddesses of Joy are represented by *The Three Graces*, seen here in a monument dedicated to Mozart in Dresden, Germany. These dancing figures are often exhibiting jubilance, comfortable with their naked bodies and in love with life. The Graces were known as the charities, gifts for which we can be grateful (in Latin, the *Gratiae*). One of these grace-full and joy-full Goddesses is Euphrosyne, the Goddess of Good Cheer and Merriment and whose name means *Heart's Joy*.

Renowned Italian Renaissance artist Sandro Botticelli painted *La Primavera* which includes these beautiful graces who appear to be celebrating spring. Other great artists throughout the centuries have also been inspired to paint these Goddesses, among them Rubens in the 1600s, as well as Picasso in the early 1900s.

The Roman Goddess of Gaiety and Happiness is Laetitia. Her qualities embraced prosperity, the end reward of accomplishing desired goals and expressing one's Divine Purpose. Legends of Laetitia indicate she carried a weapon called the *hasta pura*, a "blameless spear," a spear made without iron and presented as an award. This weapon symbolized the peace and prosperity that would flourish after battles were ended.

Because experiencing joy and exhibiting enthusiasm are so strongly associated with being *on purpose* in our lives, it is valuable to mention Diana and Artemis, the Roman and Greek Goddesses. They are often pictured as huntresses, but that is a misinterpretation of their roles as protectresses of Nature. They carry bows and arrows but also pet trusting deer who stand by, as the Goddesses assure these gentle creatures that they are safe. The bow and arrow symbolize focus and clear intention, necessary to accomplish a goal or inspired purpose.

Perhaps more relevant, a purpose today is overcoming our own inner enemies, to let go of hostilities, resentment, anger or other destructive thoughts and emotions. When we achieve self-regulation and develop a more loving attitude toward ourselves and others, we find life more rewarding.

ISIS:
TRANSFORMATION

Isis, perhaps the most renowned Goddess in the Egyptian pantheon, was the sister and wife of Osiris, the first Pharoah. It was their younger brother Seth who was jealous of Osiris and schemed to kill him. After Osiris' death, it was due to the extraordinary regenerative powers of Isis that Osiris was breathed back to life and posthumously fathered Horus, their son.

According to Jules Cashford (1993), author of *The Myth of Isis and Osiris*, Osiris metaphorically represents "the life-force of Nature which dies and is reborn, or is killed and brought back to life again. Isis becomes the redemptive force of love in Nature which brings forth new life out of the old." Isis personifies the Transformative Love that brings Osiris back from death which, in turn, symbolizes the energy of spring that brings new life to the Earth following the period of dormancy imposed by winter. The myth describes Isis's tears of grief for her Beloved flowing into the Nile River which rises each spring to nurture crops; thus, all life is reborn with the resurrection of Osiris which is initiated by Isis.

Both Isis and Osiris are personifications of the earth, air and water elements which bring forth Life as well as our feelings of love for each other and all humanity. The Love of Isis has the power of transformation. It is out of her Love that disorder becomes order, evil becomes good, and death begets new life. These deities endure human experiences and transcend all adversity. Through the resurrection of Osiris, devotees realize the possibility of life after death. The allegory of *the weighing of the heart* is linked to this myth; worshipers of Isis desire to have light hearts so they can, upon their demise, enter the kingdom of Osiris, God of the Afterlife.

The Temple on the Island of Philae is dedicated to Isis. Veneration of Isis lasted for centuries, from 3000 BC to 500 AD when the last sanctuaries were destroyed and all priestesses of the Goddess were eliminated. Many of the divine qualities of Isis were then attributed to Mother Mary as Christianity was made the official religion of the Roman Empire. The seat of this religion was in Rome, and has remained the center of Catholicism, now known as the independent city-state Vatican City.

The resurrection of Jesus, Avatar of the last 2000-year Piscean Age, arises out of the myth of Osiris and his cherished Isis. The ancient gospels found in the Middle East at Nag Hamadi and Qumran add to our knowledge of the time. Joseph Campbell, in his book *Goddesses*, states:

> Isis is one of the principal models for the Madonna in the Christian tradition; this is the motif of the mother giving birth to the child without the father present, and this standard motif comes right down in later folklore and in epics.

The picture of Isis (above) holding Horus became a model for Mary holding Jesus.

Many other cultures revere Gods and Goddesses of Change and Transformation. The earlier Babylonian God Dumuzi and Goddess Inanna were believed to suffer the same fate as Osiris and Isis. Dumuzi was resurrected by his devoted Divine Complement, the Goddess Inanna. Rituals were performed to reenact Dumuzi's death and resurrection to insure the resurgence of abundant crops. Native American traditions celebrate Butterfly Maiden, who pollinates flowers and brings life to the desert each spring.

A natural extension of Joy, expressed by Freya and the Three Graces, is the celebration of Spring. Eostre, the Germanic Goddess of the Dawn and Spring, for whom the East (the direction in which the Sun rises) and Easter are named, predates the Christian celebration of Easter as the earlier festivals occurred on the Spring Equinox. The date of Easter changes each year as it is based on an ancient pagan calendar. Easter falls on the Sunday after the first full moon following the Spring Equinox. Since the Spring Equinox celebrated the return of the Sun and Life itself, it was easily adapted to celebrate the resurrection of Christ by early Christians.

It is fascinating to see how ancient cultures were able to weave their beliefs together to conform with the prevailing institutions of the time, whether governmental or religious. Transformation has deep roots. Quite literally transformation is seen in the change of seasons and the way in which humanity understands each individual's lifespan. Here we can interpret transformation as the ability to change, the ability to overcome all obstacles and to create success after failure, to learn the lessons that each challenge presents to us. When we truly comprehend our role in each life event so we no longer react adversely in similar situations, we grow in wisdom and truth, and become enlightened with healthy bodies, light hearts and peaceful minds.

MOTHER EARTH, MAWU, GAIA, OSHUN & PACHAMAMA: FEELING MOTHERED, GROUNDED & AT HOME

Many of the Goddesses we have been learning about are Mother Goddesses. We call the Earth *Mother Earth* and *Mother Nature*. Those Goddesses of the Earth important to mention here are known by other names: Gaia, Mawu, Oshun and Pachamama among others. In *Pachamama's Children*, authors Cumes and Valencia describe what the Quechuan people believe:

> It is with Her that they share life and, just as giving and taking is a basis of existence among people, so the Quechua believe they must give as well as take from Pachamama. So dependent are they on Her, so involved is the relationship, that they regard Pachamama as an extension of themselves—a being that needs taking care of—a force that must be nourished and protected lest it die.

Aeons ago humanity viewed the Earth from a limited point of view: she was flat and limited in scope. If they sailed too far sailors believed they would fall off the edge. Now, with the advent of technology, we can see that the Earth is a globe, revolving around the sun and moving through space. Antiquated beliefs seem laughable, but there was a time when people could be burned at the stake for believing an idea that contradicted the prevailing view. To avoid this fate atronomer Copernicus, whose theory that the Earth was not the center of the Universe but revolved around the Sun, delayed publishing his treatise until just before his death in 1543.

It is time to open our minds and embrace our Oneness with the Earth and with all that is. Many cultures have revered the Earth, but over time we have brought under our control Nature's elements: we have used *Fire* to cook, heat our homes, and power our vehicles; we have invented ways to defy gravity and fly through the *Air*; we have sustained ourselves by planting in the *Earth* and harvesting crops; we have developed ways to propel ourselves over and under the *Water* and transport goods so that trade reaches around the world. As we have done these things for our own benefit, we have all too often disrespected, even disregarded, the Earth Herself. This planet is a living, breathing entity that needs our nurturing in return for all that She provdes for us. The Earth must heal from the atrocities we have committed upon her. We can be the instruments for healing our Mother Earth as we express Love and Gratitude for Her and All She provides us.

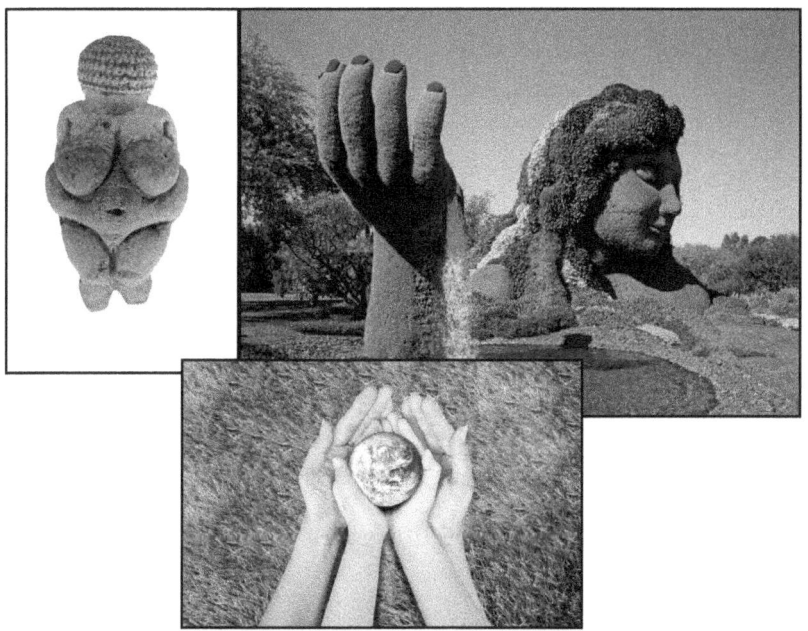

Mother Earth ~ we call her *Mother* ~ has been revered by some ancient cultures for millennia. The Venus of Willendorf, pictured here, is only four and a half inches tall. She is over 25,000 years old and now resides in Vienna, Austria. Many of these tiny statues were placed in the Earth to encourage fertility and an abundant harvest. More modern representations are in botanical gardens or in photographs circulated on social media which demonstrate our love of our Planet and her plentiful riches that provide the air we breathe, the food we eat and the water we drink. It is heartening to look at images of the Earth held in our hands, cherished and appreciated for all She gives us.

Mother Nature is comprised of Elements: Ether, Air, Fire, Water, and Earth. Each element is distinctive and is worthy of our acknowledgement and gratitude.

I AM inextricably connected to the AIR Element.

I Breath in the oxygen, nitrogen, hydrogen
and other invisible gases.

After I exhale I wait ~ soon, an irresistible urge causes me to
Breathe in again.

I realize that LIFE is Breathing me!

The AIR and I are ONE.

I AM inextricably connected to the EARTH Element.

I walk on this Blessed Planet.

I can jump high off the ground, but, under my own power,
I cannot resist the gravitational pull of Mother Earth.

My physical body is bound to the Earth!

The EARTH and I are ONE.

I AM inextricably connected to the WATER Element.

I drink water every day.
I cannot live more than a few days without Water.

I AM grateful for this Sacred Substance which sustains my Life.

The WATER and I are One.

I AM inextricably connected to the FIRE Element.

If freezing weather descends on the location where I reside,
I cannot endure icy cold temperatures very long.

I must have enough heat to maintain mobility,
and sunshine to sustain my vitality!

The FIRE and I are ONE.

I AM inextricably connected to the ETHER Element.

I know that a gossamer aura exists around my body.

Kirlian photography reveals this precious facet of my Being.

Reports from amputees tell me that phantom pain remains
in the etheric limb after the physical limb has been removed.

I honor this invisible Etheric Energy that surrounds me.

The ETHER and I are One.

I AM MANIFESTING UNITY CONSCIOUSNESS.

AT THIS CRITICAL TIME ON PLANET EARTH,
EACH HEART AND MIND IS OPEN AND
SHARING THE QUALITIES THAT WILL
HELP EARTH ATTAIN PEACE AND
HAPPINESS FOR ALL LIFE.

HIDING IN PLAIN SIGHT: IMAGES OF THE DIVINE FEMININE

Images of the best in women have been carved, painted, etched in stone, extolled in song and written in the pages of books for centuries. Yet we have been so mired in patriarchal thinking that we have tuned them out, neither seeing nor hearing the messages they impart. This is a reminder that God has another face ~ that of woman and divine mother ~ and she has been hiding in plain sight for hundreds of years.

Even the Holy Trinity has been coopted to represent only the Divine Masculine. In Truth, it is a symbol of Father God, Mother God (the Holy Spirit) and the Son/Daughter of God. It is an emblem of the Divine Family, the Best in each of us, the Union of the qualities of the Creative Source that gave birth to Humanity.

Each of us is comprised of masculine and feminine attributes. Let us appreciate the signs and wonders of our Goddess heritage, and see with new eyes the beauty and truth of who we are.

LIBERTY
FREEDOM
JUSTICE
VISTORY

Images of
Divine Feminine
Hiding
in plain sight

Four of my favorite Goddesses are those that stand in prominent places in the United States. We see Lady Liberty holding her torch high in New York Harbor but we often disregard what she stands for. She is an symbol of the Liberty granted to each of us by virtue of our citizenship in this country. Nowhere else is democracy upheld, indeed celebrated, as it is in the United States of America. This goddess welcomes those seeking the independence to express their sacred beliefs and pursue their goals.

STATUE OF LADY LIBERTY

GODDESS OF FREEDOM ON THE CAPITOL DOME

The Goddess of Freedom graces the top the Capitol Dome in Washington D. C. She is often overlooked and her message missed. She also symbolizes the Freedom citizens of the United States have to enjoy their rights without being oppressed by dictators or totalitarian governments that the daily news reports imprison and literally kill anyone who disagrees with their policies. The Capitol Building itself is a Temple, a sacred site which suggests to all visitors that the government of this great country insures Freedom from oppression.

STATUE OF CONTEMPLATION
HOLDING THEMIS, GODDESS OF JUSTICE
UNITED STATES SUPREME COURT BUILDING

The Goddess of Divine Justice is held in the hand of the Statue of Contemplation on the steps of the Supreme Court Building in Washington D. C. She is blindfolded, representing the quality of justice free of biases, prejudices or preconceived beliefs that would prevent honest outcomes to judicial proceedings. She holds a scale on which evidence can be weighed, balancing both sides of any disagreement and showing us that, in fairness, each side will be respected.

GODDESS OF VICTORY
FIRST DIVISION MEMORIAL IN PRESIDENT'S PARK, WASHINGTON D.C.

This statue of the Goddess of Victory stands in Washington D. C. in President's Park and signifies the victory we achieved in World War I. Other magnificent statues are the Winged Victory in the Louvre in Paris and Victoria, Roman Goddess of Victory, in Rome driving a quadriga, a chariot drawn by four horses, on top of the Italian Palace of Justice. Statues of Goddesses appear in virtually every state and every country around the world and are revered for the qualities they represent: Power, Grace, Wisdom, Love, Peace and more.

WHAT'S A GODDESS TO DO?

The symbolism of the Goddess has taken on an electrifying power for modern women. The rediscovery of the ancient matrifocal civilizations has given us a deep sense of pride in woman's ability to create and sustain culture. It has exposed the falsehoods of patriarchal history, and given us models of female strength and authority. The Goddess—ancient and primeval; the first of deities; patroness of the Stone Age hunt and of the first sowers of seeds; under whose guidance the herds were tamed, the healing herbs first discovered; in whose image the first works of art were created; for whom the standing stones were raised; who was the inspiration of song and poetry—is recognized once again in today's world. She is the bridge, on which we can cross the chasms within ourselves, which were created by our social conditioning, and reconnect with our lost potentials. She is the ship, on which we sail the waters of the deep self, exploring the uncharted seas within. She is the door, through which we pass into the future. She is the cauldron, in which we who have been wrenched apart simmer until we again become whole. She is the vaginal passage, through which we are born.

This passage from *The Spiral Dance* inspires us to *know that we know*. Within us, as women, we have all the "strength and authority," wisdom, love and power to recreate ourselves - to become the best that we have the potential to be.

We learned to think and feel the way we do about ourselves by how we were treated by others. If we were wanted, loved without conditions, treated with kindness and respect, we learned that we are appreciated for who we are - not for what we do or how we behave. We learned by having our needs met in a timely way that we are safe and that the world is one we can trust. Our lives - and all of our relationships - are then based on this belief system.

If we were treated badly, if we were neglected, abused, severely criticized or made to feel bad about ourselves, those imprints are still in our cells. As many trauma therapists like Dr. Robert Scaer (2004) contend in his book of the same title, *The Body Bears the Burden.*

What is most important to understand is that this conditioning process formed our egos. The ego is often defined as a person's sense of self-esteem. This Freudian concept of ego distinguishes between our instinctive responses that occur at an unconscious level and those determined at a conscious level by our higher brain functions.

We can see this process occurring when we interact with a child. Children are eager to learn, virtually ravenous for new experiences. They gobble up life and want to sample everything. Each experience becomes encoded in their brains and bodies so they build expectations that what they encounter represents how the world works. As they form opinions about the workings of the world, their coping strategies, adaptations, and survival skills are interpreted as the *right* way. After all, whatever they did worked! They survived!

Now they have a tool the ego will use in new circumstances that are similar to the first circumstance. Children anticipate that new experiences will be like those in which the tools they used were applied. In fact, the child expects that life is consistent and predictable. They create a program within their brains/minds that says, "I survived and learned in this particular way, now I can do it again."

Whatever we learned as children, especially what we concluded based on how we were treated, becomes our *programming*, the default settings in our computer-like brains. Then we go about living our lives from the unconscious, deeply instilled patterns of thought and feeling, rarely questioning what shows up. It seems like we have nothing to do with what happens, unaware that we are cause, not effect. We have no conscious awareness that our expectations, the programs hidden in the recesses of our brains/minds/bodies, are influencing what shows up in our lives!

As we grow up we develop an ego that is operating on faulty data, on misperceptions and the acceptance of other people's beliefs about us and about life itself. Our egos think we are the limited individuals that others told us we were. We have accepted as true a view of ourselves that is generally self-critical rather than self-loving. Our self-esteem is damaged, maybe even non-existent since our self-perception is one of unworthiness. How could we be loveable ~ or even worthy of love ~ when others have been telling us how flawed and inadequate we are?

When we are constantly concerned about what others think about us, we go about our lives attempting to please others. We are taught that taking care of others and not thinking about ourselves, which is considered selfish, is the best way to live. It can be gratifying to help others, but the cost can be high if we neglect ourselves. We can suffer ill health: physically, mentally, emotionally and spirituality.

Our lives are full of paradoxes, concepts that seem contradictory. We may have difficulty reconciling self-care and caring for others. We live in a world of duality and we often think in terms of polar opposites; therefore, if someone disagrees with our views we enter into an "I'm right and you're wrong" dynamic. Self-care is primary. If we do not care for ourselves, we use ourselves up. Like a bank account that spends all its capital and never earns any interest, soon it is empty.

Nathaniel Branden, known as the "Father of the Self-Esteem Movement" states that "our self-esteem is rooted internally." More, in Brandon's words, self-esteem is:

1. Confidence in our ability to think and to cope with the basic challenges of life.
2. Confidence in our right to be happy, the feeling of being worthy, deserving, entitled to assert our needs and wants and to enjoy the fruits of our efforts.

Caroline Myss, a motivational speaker, asks, "How would your life change if your self-esteem improved?" Is the language you use when you talk to yourself patient, kind, loving, and supportive? Probably not! Most of our internal messages are reiterations of what others told us so now we hear in our own voice, the voice of someone who said we were not good enough, not lovable, not perfect. Admonitions drive our lives as our egos continue to tell us not to change because we survived when we first experienced the old situations. We know how to handle those.

Paradoxically, at deep inner levels we expect the same treatment that we have always gotten so we inadvertently set up situations to prove that our conclusions are RIGHT! We are unlovable. We're damaged goods. How could anyone love us?

What a dilemma! How do we go about changing a belief system that does not want to change. Our egos tell us it is protecting us. Remember, when you were a child, you coped ~ you survived by working out a strategy. Whatever your tactic was, crying out in fear or sadness, striking out in anger, acting out in confusion or other autonomic nervous system response, your particular mode of responding became deeply ingrained in your cells. It helped you survive before, so it is a tried and true method that worked.

Now well established, these programs are not easily changed. An unknown, unproven strategy, no matter how appealing on a conscious level, might not work. When the fear that once caused us to do whatever we did is triggered, our body/mind, our nervous system, and, of course, our ego, will do what it has always done. On a conscious level we may desire to have better results in our lives, but on a subconscious level our knee-jerk reactions are still generating the same disappointing, disheartening results we have always gotten. How could it be otherwise? The program is a belief that these results are all we can expect!

Einstein to reputed to have said that doing the same thing over and over expecting a different result is *insanity*. No wonder most of us struggle through life. We know that a house divided (our subconscious and conscious minds) cannot stand. Our subconscious programming mandates that we are unworthy while our conscious minds desire to be loved ~ to know we are worthy of love.

We really need to go back to the beginning. Through self-reflection and self-examination we can see clearly how we were treated, how we adapted; and we must love ourselves free from those old limiting patterns, those thoughts, feelings and actions that no longer serve us.

Our egos formed with the knowledge and wisdom we had at the time. We don't need to fight it. A better way is to *reprogram* it; enroll it in the service of our greater good now. To paraphrase Maya Angelou: "Now that we know better, we can do better."

How do we start? Let's begin by bringing our attention to the qualities the Goddesses have been modeling for aeons. Each Goddess expresses all of the values but exemplifies one or more particular quality we can begin to perceive as our own. We can see that the Goddesses have been waiting to be called upon as we transcend our egos and honor the Divine within us. That connection to the Goddess within, long forgotten, frees us to overcome any challenges we are facing and become the best we have ever been. So we will address particular virtues, exploring ways we can awaken to their Presence within us.

After each Virtue that includes an explanation of how we got off track and forgot who we are, there will be several easy-to-do exercises that you can choose among to create the results you desire in your life. None is hard, nor do any take a great deal of time. You are awakening to who you are at the Heart of your Being. Your own awareness will help you choose which ones work for you. Your reluctant ego will ultimately cooperate to assist in the process of becoming your Best YOU! It will acquiesce to your True Self and you can shine your Light with Power, Wisdom and Love.

I AM EXPRESSING MY TRUTH & MY POWER

While I was writing this section of *Girls, Goddesses & Growing Up* the 2024 Olympic Games were being played in Paris, France. If you are looking for models of powerful women, watch the women of the gymnastic teams on YouTube. Of course, I fell in love with the girls/women of the United States' team who won the team competition and a gold medal! Noting a positive cultural shift in the field of gymnastics, gold medalist Simone Biles, said, "We're going to put in the work, and we're going to show the results. We don't have to be put in a box anymore." Simone demonstrated the Power of speaking our Truth as well as the realization that women are worthy of respect.

At four feet eight inches tall, how could this petite woman model *power*? What did the members of this extraordinary team, women from 16 (the youngest age allowed to compete) to 27 (the oldest U. S. Olympic gymnast in 72 years), do that showed audiences around the world their power? What did Simone mean when she said women competitors didn't have to be put in a box anymore?

With enormous discipline and self-control the Olympic contenders demonstrated their determination, passion, courage, grace under stressful circumstances, and the willingness to stand up and show the world the results of their hard work. My heart sings as I reflect on these marvelous young women.

Let me ask you, do you feel powerful? Do you stand in the Truth of who you are? These are big questions. Maybe our Olympic gymnasts are providing the inspiration to answer these questions.

Let's first consider the definition of power. Power is defined as the ability to do something. That sounds innocuous enough but there is another meaning that implies an ability of others, individuals or whole societies, to exert control over people and entire populations. David Hawkins, author of *Power vs Force*, describes ideal power coming from "unrevealed sources" [perhaps Heavenly sources] over which we have no control. Further, he distinguishes between power and force, saying:

Because power is effortless it goes unseen and unsuspected. Force is experienced through the senses; power can be recognized only through inner awareness. . . . Force always moves against something, whereas power does not move against anything. Force is incomplete and therefore has to constantly be fed energy. Power is total and complete in itself and requires nothing from outside itself. It makes no demands; it has no needs. Because force has an insatiable appetite, it constantly consumes. Power, in contrast, energizes, gives forth, supplies and supports. Power gives life and energy. Force takes these away. We notice that power is associated with compassion and makes us feel positively about ourselves. Force is associated with judgment and makes us feel badly about ourselves.

To me, Dr. Hawkins is equating Power with Divine Energy derived from our Creative Source. That leads me to our Breath. It is known that human beings can survive for a few weeks without food, only a few days without water and only minutes without oxygen. You can fast without food or water for a period of time, but you cannot hold your breath for more than moments. Breath *is* life. Hawkins is telling us that Power is an unseen energy that sustains us ~ like the Breath. We can think of the Breath as the channel for conducting into our bodies a current of Life Energy, Aliveness, Vitality and, in Eastern terms, the flow of Chi or Prana.

The Olympic gymnasts expressed their power through their movements. *Expression*, according to Dr. Dorothy Gates, founder of the *SpectraDynamics* program, "is the direct and orderly release of emotional energy." She explains that when we think of something ~ when we feel an urge ~ we release that energy by expressing it. We are designed by Nature to do that, but often we suppress that energy.

Suppression sidetracks our energy into another direction. For example, I think I'll write, I'll work on my book this morning, but I get distracted and do something else. When I suppress this urge often enough, it becomes a habit and my body/mind automatically represses my desire to write and finds other things to do.

Repression is the unconscious "restraint, prevention, or inhibition of a feeling." Repression may have been promoted in our families of origin. When we were growing up we might have had the feeling that we wanted to go outside and play, but our parents said that we could play later, after chores were done. In our adulthood we might have a desire to be creative, but we tell ourselves that there are chores to be done, phone calls to make, errands to run, appointments to keep ad infinitum. We get distracted without even realizing this habit has taken over our creative impulses. We tell ourselves that we'll do it later ~ and later never comes. We can postpone expressing our talents, our passion, our joy, for a lifetime, disappointing ourselves as we adhere to old dictates.

Impressions are made in our brain/bodies very early in our development. They have been called imprints, what my dear friend and colleague Barbara Findeisen called *lasting impressions*, and they influence our lives without our awareness. We are operating out of old conditioning. We suppress and repress our creativity, our desire to be unique and make our contribution to the world instead of expressing who we genuinely are. Again, our parents and care providers did the best they could, but it is time to break the chains of old programming that told us to conform, to deny our individuality and to just get along with others' ideas of how to think, feel, and act.

Thinking is a powerful activity in itself. Our thoughts, which we think are our own, are usually derived from what those around us, especially our parents, teachers, physicians, and other authority figures tell us. I listen to my precious three-year-old great-granddaughter make pronouncements like "take your shoes off," when I go to her house. Taking shoes off is a rule that will be universal for her until she learns that other people do not always take their shoes off when entering their homes. Ask yourself, what rules did you learn that are still running your life? I've found that eating everything on my plate is an old program surfacing very late in my life. My father made a real point of this when I was a kid. I'm sure he would be pleased to know that I clean up my plate now, something I rebelled against as a child. Now I need to discern whether it is really good for me to clean up my plate. If I'm just heeding an old program, I could leave a few bites for the angels, as Dolly Parton advises.

When I did research on aging while I was in college I found that older people return to what they learned when they were children. Religiosity, that is the belief in a particular religion, was a subject I was interested in. I wondered if people became more spiritual as they aged. What the research revealed was that older adults most often return to the religious principles they were taught as children. Those beliefs are comfortable and easily accessed in their neural networks. Integrating new philosophies late in life that could challenge beliefs implanted long ago is not likely.

There is an old adage: "As a man [or woman] thinketh, so he [she] is." Dr. Gates told her students, "You think, you think!" The unfortunate thing is that we don't know what we are thinking on a subconscious level or whose ideas we are expressing we think are our own. What are those neurons doing in the recesses of our brains that act like the unseen programs in our computers? We fall back on implicit (hidden) memories that are driving our behaviors now.

Many experts today, as well as philosophers and religious sages over the centuries, have told us that what we are thinking is causing us to suffer. Changing negative thinking can be liberating. On a conscious level that sounds like it will work, but does it get to the real cause of our distress? Where do the negative thoughts come from? And, if we don't address the underlying cause, will the same issues keep surfacing in our lives? Changing our thoughts is clearly part of the solution, but those changes must be repeated often; after all, it took years to implant them in the first place. Over time new programming will replace old erroneous ideas, but calling upon your Higher Self ~ your notion of God within ~ to assist you in transmuting that destructive energy can speed your process and eliminate the underlying causes whether you are aware of them on a conscious level or not.

Maybe none of us has an original thought because the majority of what we think is derived from what others have told us, what we have read in books or heard from authority figures or the media. Some of the ideas are so ingrained in our culture that to disagree is to evoke criticism, censure and disbelief. In the *Forward* to *Childbirth and Authoritative Knowledge,* Rayna Rapp credits Brigitte Jordan with coining the term *authoritative knowledge.* Rapp says, "authoritative knowledge isn't produced simply by access to complex technology, or an abstract will to hierarchy. It is a way of organizing power relations in a room that makes them seem literally unthinkable in any other way." The assumption that the knowledge espoused within our institutions, whether those are academic, medical, economic, governmental or political, is Truth is being exposed to reveal its biases and prejudices. The motivation of many organizations and individuals is to control others and to make money, therefore, principles, beliefs, and even the terminology used must be preserved to exert authority (force, according to David Hawkins) and insure profits.

Let's look at the language we use every day. This is in English, but the concepts can apply in any language. Shakespeare asked this famous question in his play *Hamlet*: "to be or not to be, that is the question." It's a question about living or dying. The passive verb *be* is conjugated:

I am	We are
You are	You are (plural)
He, she or it is	They are

I wrote about this in my first book *The Renaissance of Birth: Changing the Language of Childbirth.* It may seem silly to be examining the grammar we use every day, but these are *power-full* phrases. Every time you think or utter "I am" you are mentally commanding your brain to accept whatever follows "I am." The verb *be*, in the form of *am* or *are,* is like an equals sign. If you say "I am sick. I am tired. I am angry. I am frustrated," your obedient brain will take those instructions literally. But, you say, "I didn't mean that!" Your brain does not know the difference between what you mean and what you don't. It is your faithful servant and will manifest whatever you focus on. Repeated often enough these expressions will make impressions on your neurology and physiology. So, you get to be *right*, as your body expresses illness, fatigue, anger, frustration ~ all those things you say you are. The real point here is to turn those statements into affirmations for the best in yourself: "I am healthy," "I am full of energy," "I am happy," and "I am content."

In 2000 Barbara Hoberman Levine published *Your Body Believes Every Word You Say.* She was motivated to write this book because she had been dealing with a brain tumor. As she collected suggestions of better ways to think and speak about her health, she noted:

> When I am afraid because I believe I may have an illness, my thoughts put my body into a state of agitation and unrest, conditions that support the appearance of disease. But, if I believe I am healthy, I will find evidence to support that belief.

Louise L. Hay wrote *You Can Heal Your Life* after overcoming childhood trauma. She concluded her book with a list of disorders which she intuited were the *probable causes* of various diseases followed by her suggestions for *new thought patterns.* For example, acne, a common skin condition that clogs pores and causes outbreaks is the result of "not accepting the self. Dislike of the self." The new thought patterns are "*I am a Divine expression life. I love and accept myself where I am right now."* Yeast infections are caused by "denying your own needs. Not supporting yourself." The words that heal are "*I now choose to support myself in loving, joyous ways.*"

Not only can words support or sabotage our health and well-being, we can project them to others. "You are mean" versus "You are kind and compassionate" impacts the energy field of the person to whom you make your comments. Positive words can raise self-esteem while negative words can cause self-doubt or a defensive reaction. Newberg and Waldman, authors of *Words Can Change Your Brain*, state:

> Language shapes our behavior, and each word we use is imbued with multitudes of personal meaning. The right words, spoken in the right way, can bring us love, money, and respect, while the wrong words—or even the right words spoken in the wrong way—can lead a country to war. We must carefully orchestrate our speech if we want to achieve our goals and bring our dreams to fruition.

This is particularly important to remember when we are talking to children. We are shaping their behavior and self-image with our words. Children believe what big people say. Maybe you still recall the words an adult said to you that made you feel really good about yourself ～ or really bad. These messages pour into the subconscious mind where they accumulate and are expressed in our actions and reactions well into our adult lives. Substitute positive life-affirming words every time you catch yourself using language that drains your power. You are using your Life Breath every time you speak! You are creating with your words. What words do you really desire to manifest results in your life and, of course, the lives of those around you?

Our model for expressing our Power and speaking our Truth is Pallas Athena. Holding a spear, as she does in the image shown earlier, she appears armed and ready for battle. However, she uses the power of her wits and wisdom to solve problems. Her Presence exudes power and inner strength. Our Olympic gymnasts exhibited this power in their performances in Paris. No longer in a box of society's expectations that women are weak or overly emotional, these young women showed the world what it looks like to be a Goddess of the New Age.

Exercises you can do daily to cultivate your Power are Breathing *The Balanced Breath*, *Watching Your Words*, and making *I Am Statements* that reprogram your subconscious mind to think the best of you.

THE BALANCED BREATH

I breathe in, counting to four.
I hold the breath in, counting to four.
I exhale, courting to four.
I hold the breath out, counting to four.

I repeat this breath several times,
while being grateful for each breath.

The Power of the Source flows through me with each breath.

In *The Four Agreements* Don Miguel Ruiz tells us that "the most important agreements are the ones you made with yourself. In these agreements you tell yourself who you are, what you feel, what you believe, and how to behave." The first agreement ~ *Be impeccable with your word* ~ is first because "regardless of what language you speak, your intent manifests through the word."

WATCHING MY WORDS

I am vigilant, watching the words I speak.
I know "In the Beginning is the Word,"
and my words are creative.

I no longer use self-deprecating expressions
when I am thinking or talking about myself.

I now choose loving thoughts and words
to validate my love and acceptance of myself.

No more do I repeat old views that I am unworthy.

I AM whole, worthy and infinitely lovable.

I KNOW THE TRUTH OF WHO I AM.

**I AM RADIATING THE SAPPHIRE BLUE LIGHT OF
DIVINE POWER.**

WORD SUBSTITUTION

I no longer use the word *try*, a failure word.
I substitute the word *attempt*.

I no longer say "*I'm sorry*" when I have done nothing wrong.
I stop apologizing for myself.
I say "*I regret*" when I err, or ask "*Please excuse me.*"

I use the word *hope* sparingly
as it has a connotation of doubt and dread.

I have feared that my hope would not be realized,
therefore, I now substitute the word *trust*,
knowing that the best outcome is possible.

POWER VISUALIATION

Becoming relaxed, more and more relaxed, I close my eyes and envision Sunshine-Gold Light pouring forth from the Heart of the Cosmos. This Golden Radiance beams into the top of my head and slowly fills my head, my neck, my shoulders, my arms, hands and fingers. This Divine Illumination travels down my torso, into my solar plexus, my pelvis, my back, hips, thighs, knees, calves, ankles, feet and toes until every cell in my body feels the glow of the Golden Light. I scan my body for any areas that seem dark and allow the Light to illuminate those places as well. It takes only moments to appreciate this Light, this Life, this empowerment of each cell to ignite my sense of personal power. I am a powerful Being of Light, and I go about my day radiating Light to all I meet. Taking a deep Light-filled breath, I resume my activities renewed, restored and revitalized.

I AM THE LIGHT.

I AM ACCESSING MY OWN WISDOM

Wisdom embraces a number of similar qualities including enlightenment, illumination and understanding. The color associated with Wisdom is Sunshine Yellow so it is easy to envision Light illuminating you, glowing from within your heart center as well as radiating from the Heavens to surround and fill your body and mind. If you regard yourself as Spiritual, you are probably a seeker of Enlightenment.

According to the online version of the *Encyclopedia Britannica*, enlightenment can simply mean "to have knowledge or understanding." But it can also mean "a state of heightened awareness, profound inner peace, and a deep understanding of the interconnectedness of all life." This form of enlightenment provides the sense of *Peace* that passes all understanding. It transcends our limited view of ourselves as just human beings, and expands our awareness to see ourselves as spiritual beings interconnected, interrelated, and interdependent with all life. We are made in the image of God, therefore, we are expressions of our Father/Mother God on Earth. We have an element of the Divine within us, no matter how it may have become obscured by recalcitrant egos dedicated to gratifying our senses and keeping us in a rut.

In our Western society we consider mental attributes like wisdom and the acquisition of knowledge to be associated with the left brain and predominantly masculine. However, other valuable mental capacities such as intuition and imagination are associated with the right brain and are feminine in nature. Intuition is often ignored or scorned because it seems to arise from an inner awareness that is not tangible. A skeptic might ask, "Where's your evidence? Where's the proof?"

Historically, insights believed to have been inspired by a muse or experienced as an epiphany were highly regarded, but over time knowledge that appeared to arise from intuition was questioned and might even have been considered to have come from a demonic source. This line of thinking and questioning devalued women's intuition and imagination along with women themselves as patriarchal values predominated cultures around the world.

The right brain is considered emotional; indeed, there are more connections to the limbic area of brain from the right hemisphere. As the scientific method, which values concrete evidence, has become more and more relied upon, objectivity is prized over subjectivity. It is easy to see how women, emotions, intuition, imagination and other characteristics associated with the right brain and femininity have been devalued.

In *Intuition: The Inside Story*, contributing author Charles Laughlin states:

Intuition typically labels a type of experience, in which the answer to a question, the solution to a problem, guidance in following some goal, a creative impulse resulting in the emergence of some image, idea or pattern, springs into consciousness whole-cloth as it were, seemingly out of nowhere.

In the same book, *Intuition*, Evelyn H. Monsay says,

Imagination is a form of thought associated with mental images. Imagination typically refers to the appearance of images in the mind, sometimes intuitively received, which can be manipulated and require translation into words.... Imagination shares the global, nonrational nature of intuition and is a close cousin to it.

Monsay looks to the future saying "We are the emotionally involved thinker whose imagination is fueled with intuitive notions of realities yet to be developed in the reason of tomorrow." What she described in 1997 is truer a quarter century later. This vision calls upon the harmonization of our right and left brains to appreciate objective *and* subjective approaches, mental *and* emotional capabilities as well as the union of what have been considered masculine and feminine attributes within each of us.

Sophia, our model of Wisdom, has been idolized in myth, art and sculpture. Sophia, the Voice of God as Co-creator in the Old Testament, has represented the Feminine Face of God. Yet religions across nations and cultures today still deny the Goddess, the Mother aspect of the Divine. It may take time for devotees to embrace the Feminine Nature of God, but women can begin *now* to claim their divine heritage. Both science and scripture have acknowledged the Divine Feminine. Even without this acknowledgment from established institutions, individual girls and women can respect their brains/minds, emotions, intuition, imaginations, creativity and procreativity.

The awareness of mind/body integration that began in the mid-twentieth century opened the way to accepting and appreciating both aspects of our being. With the aid of electronic equipment, the vibrations of our brains were able to be measured in hertz or cycles per second (cps). This revealed that in different states of consciousness, that is, awake, asleep, in meditation or dreaming, our brain wave frequencies vary. What is significant about this is that we can teach ourselves to access those different vibrational frequencies and take advantage of the best that can accomplished in each state.

Brain wave states are Beta, 13-35 cps, Alpha, 8-13 cps, Theta 4-8 cps and Delta, .5-4 cps. In Beta we are awake and are able to problem-solve. In Alpha we are in a relaxed state; in Theta we experience periods of creativity, daydreaming, and fantasizing; and in Delta we are in deep sleep. Subsequent to discovering these four states of consciousness, accomplished meditators have been studied and Gamma waves (greater than 35 cps) have been identified. This is a heightened state of awareness.

Below is a chart that compares the brain wave frequencies at the different states of awareness. We go through these states naturally each day and night. The Mayo Clinic and many other organizations are teaching people to use biofeedback as a mind-body technique to control body functions, such as "heart rate, breathing patterns and muscle responses."

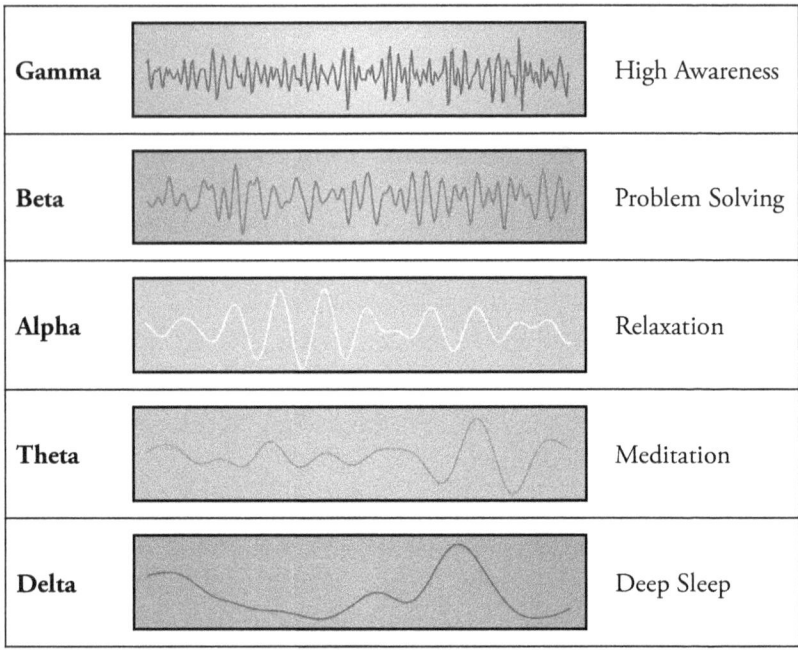

Gamma		High Awareness
Beta		Problem Solving
Alpha		Relaxation
Theta		Meditation
Delta		Deep Sleep

What is most relevant is that the Alpha brain wave state can be accessed to change programming. Alpha is a portal to changing your mind! It is easy to do and can be done entirely under your control. Once you learn to enter an Alpha state of consciousness on your own, you can reprogram you brain/mind to accept those ideas that you determine will improve the quality of your life!

REPROGRAMMING MYSELF

Before you start to reprogram your old beliefs, it is good to look at the results you are currently getting in your life. Like a mirror, the world reflects to us how we feel about ourselves. On a scale of 0 – 10 rate your responses to these questions:

1. Are my relationships loving and rewarding?
2. Is my career successful?
3. Do I have plenty of money?
4. Do I feel *on purpose* in my life?
5. Am I accountable for my choices or do I blame others or myself, and feel resentful, guilty or ashamed when things go wrong?

If every answer is not a 10, you have areas of your life that you can improve. Would you like a better relationship? A more satisfying career? Abundance? A feeling of being on purpose in your life? Would you like to be more accountable instead of feeling like a victim, or humiliated when things seem to go wrong? The Dalai Lama has said, "When you think everything is someone else's fault, you will suffer a lot. When you realize that everything springs only from yourself, you will learn both peace and joy."

I began reprogramming myself decades ago. The good news is that I have made a lot of progress. I also still have more work to do! I have used with great success a program that was called *SpectraDynamics*, newly improved and renamed *Presence of Mind LLC*. I have studied *PSYCH-K*, which has been endorsed by Bruce Lipton, and gets excellent results. With clients, I frequently use *Eye Movement Desensitization and Reprocessing* (EMDR). There are also many CDs available to help you access the various states of consciousness.

It is important to understand that accessing altered states of consciousness is normal. You go through these states naturally. Most often you do so without realizing it. You naturally go through several periods of Alpha during the night as you sleep. These sleep cycles allow your brain to process and organize information before you awaken the next day. This is one reason humans cannot go without sleep.

Sleep is a gift granted by Mother Nature. As an example, after watching a disturbing movie, you could activate specific processing for your brain/mind to perform during sleep. In this case you would program your biocomputer to pay special attention to processing any fright or disturbance you felt. It's as easy as saying "I release tension and anxiety while I sleep. When I awaken in the morning I am refreshed and renewed." With that focus you awaken with fewer images and memories of the *disturbances* you witnessed. It is liberating to know how your mind works.

The brain/mind does not know the difference between what is real and what is imaged, so if life has presented experiences that were frightening, those old memories can be processed in a similar way. To prove this to yourself think of a time when you were awakened during the night by a dream that you had fallen out of bed. Your body responded as if you really had fallen, because it did not know that you only imagined it.

Your Alpha mind is a master at following your instructions. It functions below your conscious awareness, but you can give it a command and it will carry it out to perfection. This is done with affirmations, but it can take some time and numerous repetitions to overwrite a lifetime of negative thinking. And returning to your old critical self-talk during the rest of your day will counteract your efforts to reprogram yourself.

Alpha is simply a slower brain wave frequency that you can access with practice. It is a relaxed state that enhances your wellbeing if you just take a 20-minute *power nap*. What is not well known is that you can recite an affirmation before your nap and your brain will process that statement while you are in the relaxed alpha state just as it does when you are sleeping at night. If you go into this relaxed state several times a day you greatly enhance the benefits you receive.

The greatest benefits are derived from focusing on one subject for a period of time, then working on another. You are reeducating your brain/mind to eliminate tension at the same time you are teaching it to increase your love of yourself. Like magic, you will discover that your love for yourself is reflected in the love that returns to you.

Who would have thought that relaxing, letting go of stress and repeating loving thoughts about ourselves, our wellbeing, our worthiness to receive prosperity, perfect health, caring relationships, and all the goodness we can imagine would be the answer to our prayers?

Our upbringing has taught us just the opposite! We have been browbeaten to perform, to believe we have to, ought to, should, must ~ the list of demands is endless. When I first started examining my own self talk I discovered I was starting each day with my mental list of *have-tos*. I *have to* do this, and *ought to* do that. I was sabotaging all the joy out of my life. I have had to use my alpha sessions, my power naps, to change this old program to start the day with the bright expectation of a child: ***I get to; I look forward to; I have the opportunity to; I can!***

The thoughts and the language we use can change the way we start our day, and ultimately our lives. Whatever is on our agenda is now an opportunity instead of drudgery. Our attitude becomes one of gratitude. We are thankful for life, not viewing it as demanding us to do things we resent. The more we tackle small tasks with enthusiasm, the more greater opportunities open up for us. We begin to notice the synchronies that occur. It begins to feel like the Universe is supporting us instead of placing obstacles in our path. We no longer need to beat ourselves up to accomplish our goals; we realize that the tools of transformation are the brain waves we can now harness to create a life of success and ease. Really? Yes, really!

I recommend you find a program like Presence of Mind LLC, or PSYCH-K to teach you ways to access your latent faculties. You can use your brain/mind in much more constructive ways than you have been. Our conditioning has lulled us into believing that we are helpless and hopeless, sinners from the beginning of time forever doomed to lives of struggle and pain. We buy lots of products and services to feel better about ourselves. Now you can invest in yourself to take advantage of resources you have had within you from your inception.

So begin now to plan to relax at least once a day. Take a 20-minute break at lunch, or a 20-minute nap when you get home in the evening. You are worth it!

Consistently use a word like "relax" to tell your mind what you want it to do. After a couple of weeks of making relaxation a part of your routine, just like regularly eating meals, exercising, or going to work, you will automatically start to look forward to those sessions that recharge your batteries, increase your energy and clear your mind. Tell your over-active beta mind to "be still." You deserve to have a few quiet moments without brain chatter continually telling you to do things. You will do them better after this respite.

At first you may find that your brain/mind resists relaxing, but tell it *it has a new job to do.* It must allow your Alpha mind to work silently on enhancing your well-being while you are physically relaxing. What could be easier?

When you are relaxing regularly each day, place an affirmation in your mind for your subconscious Alpha mind to process during the next few minutes. What attribute do you feel is most important to address? If you are having health issues use an affirmation like "I am at ease in my life;" or "I am in perfect health; or "I am feeling better every day." Your mind may object and tell you that it's not true, but your thoughts can now help you bring about a different reality.

Perhaps you would like more money. You may have been conditioned with phrases like "I can't afford that." You may have been encouraged to believe that money is evil. The "love of money" is what the ancient admonition advises us to avoid. This means that an obsession for money, the fear of poverty, the attitude that getting money at any cost is acceptable are all erroneous. Money is energy and all that you require is yours as you turn your attention to your worthiness ~ your love of yourself.

So a prosperity affirmation might be "I am financially free;" or "I am receiving the best life has to offer." Before you relax choose an affirmation that supports your desire and allow your Alpha mind to impress this idea into your brain/mind. It will, over time, overwrite the old admonitions that you are not worthy and not good enough to be prosperous. Be patient. Alpha is your silent friend and will help you accomplish your every desire. How fun to communicate with a part of your mind that won't talk back!

If you think about the letter Alpha ~ A or α ~ it signifies the beginning. Biblically, Alpha is the beginning and Omega is the Ending. Everything you do begins with relaxation. It initiates a cycle that stores your energy which leads to your expressing that energy as an activity. It is important to be clear to align your intention with your expression of energy. When we get distracted and do something other than what we intended, we create tension in our bodies. Our Beta idea and our alpha-directed expression are then in conflict. The idea to do something is created in your Beta level of consciousness while the energy to carry out your intention is stored in your Alpha level of consciousness. The harmony between these two is essential for a tension-free life.

Make time for Alpha sessions during your busy day. It is amazing how you will feel rejuvenated and have the energy to carry out your clear intentions.

MY ALPHA TIME

I lie down and move around until I am as comfortable as possible. I breathe in and out rhythmically feeling my belly rise and fall with each breath. I tell my conscious mind to "RELAX" and this word becomes my signal to enjoy a 20-minute relaxation session. While I am relaxed my subconscious Alpha mind is absorbing new programs that enhance my wellbeing. I know perfect health. I receive the abundance and the greater good of my Father-Mother God. I am loved beyond measure and my relationships reflect my love of myself and all life. I am at peace and peace radiates out through my energy field to travel around the Earth promoting peace in all Nations. I am grateful for this exquisite time discovering the Power and Wisdom within me to accomplish my goals with ease. I am in Harmony both within and without. When I reach the completion of my relaxation session, looking forward to the next time I relax again, I awaken refreshed and invigorated.

AWAKENING MY SPIRITUAL BRAIN CENTERS

I lie on my back with my arms at my sides. I close my eyes and breathe deeply. I command my Beta mind to "Be Still." I give my Alpha mind the suggestion to "Relax." I further instruct my Alpha Mind to be receptive to the awakening of my Spiritual Brain Centers. I am aware that transformation is imminent. I place my attention on the crown of my head envisioning a golden light radiating around my head like a halo. The light enters my cranium, reaching into my pineal gland causing this pinecone-shaped gland to glow and to vibrate. The vibration awakens this Spiritual Brain Center. My pituitary and hypothalamus also begin to vibrate. I see with my inner vision a kaleidoscope of magnificent colors wafting in front of me promising visions of the New Earth and my role upon it. I hear celestial music, I smell the fragrance of sweet but unfamiliar flowers and I taste the flavor of delicious ambrosia on my lips. Manna from Heaven flows from my Spiritual Brain Centers like dripping honey and spreads throughout my body. I feel the bliss of this Heavenly Sensation comforting me. I feel I am floating on clouds. I sense the Presence of Angelic Beings who assure me

"All Is Well."

I rest in this Knowing. When my time in Alpha is complete, I awaken refreshed and enlightened, ready to carry out the Divine Plan for my life.

I AM A TRAVELER ON LIFE'S PATH

I AM ON A JOURNEY.

I HAVE A BAG WHICH CONTAINS ALL MY MEMORIES
OF THE PAST.

I HAVE A MAP THAT POINTS THE WAY TO MY
FUTURE.

TODAY, I RELEASE ALL THE SOILED LAUNDRY
FROM MY BAG.

I AFFIRM THAT I *KNOW* WHERE I AM GOING.

I AM MY AUTHENTIC SELF,
TRAVELING AN ILLUMINED PATH
OF WISDOM AND UNDERSTANDING.

**I AM ENVELOPED IN THE SUNSHINE YELLOW LIGHT
OF DIVINE ENLIGHTENMENT.**

I AM LOVING MYSELF

There is so much we need to learn about Love. There is so much more we need to learn about loving ourselves. We are asked to open our hearts, to be kind and generous to others when most of us are afraid. Our life experiences have been filled with rejection, abandonment, betrayal, humiliation, and other atrocities that cause us to be wary. We fear being hurt again. Those heart-breaking experiences leave us feeling vulnerable and unloved, even unlovable.

From our very beginnings, from conception, we are impacted by the thoughts and emotions of our parents, doctors, teachers and others who projected their agendas onto us. If we were wanted, indeed planned, we have an initial imprint of being loved and welcomed into the world. It is estimated that half of all conceptions are unintended, which means mother or father never wanted a child or did not want a child at the time. This perception is conveyed to the embryo developing in utero a sense of being unwanted, rejected, and certainly unloved. Every feeling the mother has, whether positive or negative, is impressed upon the baby growing in her womb.

We have thought that babies in the womb are unconscious, that they do not perceive anything until well after they are born; but science is revealing that this not true. Every cell is conscious and receiving information that influences the baby's development. If love is the predominant emotion in the baby's environment, the child's growth is healthier mentally, emotionally and physically than if love is absent. If mother does not want to have a child, does not have support during her pregnancy, or is afraid, her unborn child knows this and the template for the rest of the child's life is founded on a sense of being unwelcome and unworthy. This is, in my opinion, a tragedy.

Our modern childbirth practices do nothing to improve this situation. For over one hundred years physicians have been *delivering* babies. Women have been told their natural ability to give birth is defective. They acquiesce to the medical establishment out of fear that something will go wrong and either they or their baby is at risk. These fears are exacerbated by the institutions that profit from providing delivery services ~ and these institutions do not want to change.

What we are learning is that a newborn should be placed on mother's belly. *The Sacred Hour*, written about by neonatologist Raylene Phillips, is the precious first hour when the newborn and mother have uninterrupted time together. This instills a sense of well-being in both mother and child. What could be more natural than leaving these two united after the ten months the baby has known nothing but the safety and comfort of mother's body. Yes, *ten* months!

The March of Dimes, an organization that has studied prematurity for decades, tells us that the ideal term of pregnancy is 280 days, 40 weeks or ten months. Inducing birth at 39 weeks or earlier is not advisable, but the American College of Obstetricians and Gynecologists (ACOG) finds no reason not to do so. The baby's brain is experiencing enormous development in the last days and weeks in utero. This is best accomplished within mother, not a Neonatal Intensive Care Unit (NICU) or hospital nursery.

The baby, according to Nature's design, initiates labor. The release of mother's birth hormones is suppressed or impeded by modern technology when birth is induced. But it is the impact on every newborn that is of concern because the baby's attempt to initiate labor is thwarted by induction. This begins a pattern that extends throughout life: attempts to start a project and follow through can be sabotaged by the imprint that an outside force is necessary to initiate and complete a task or accomplish a goal.

This result can be observed in children who have been born by Cesarean Section. Psychologically it is inhibiting to have the first effort in life to respond to a biological urge to begin an action subverted by outside interference. The internalization of this event impacts every tendency to take the initiative. The expectation becomes a belief that something or someone else is needed to start and complete tasks and that the body cannot be trusted to provide the signals to begin a venture.

Taking babies away from mother immediately after they are born is anathema. The cord should be left intact until it has stopped pulsing. Cutting it prematurely can precipitate breathing issues that then require resuscitation. Forcing a bulb syringe into the baby's tender throat passage can create an aversion to nursing. The more we intervene, the more we generate reasons to keep intervening.

Weighing and measuring can be postponed and nursing can be encouraged because there is a window of opportunity during the first hour after birth in which the newborn (undrugged by the effects of an epidural) will crawl unassisted to mother's breast and latch on. This instinct is overridden by procedures that remove baby from mother to perform tasks that could be done later.

Gay Hendricks, author of *Learning to Love Yourself*, notes the adverse effects of the birth process which shape our sense that something is wrong with us! Millions of children have been born in hospitals and it can be years before symptoms are displayed that might represent after-effects of birth trauma. But removal from mother immediately after being born *is* traumatic. So are all the other interventions that have become so commonplace. We have been told that a baby's lusty cries just mean she has strong lungs, not that the cries are indications of the baby's distress. No wonder we have trouble finding our voices and expressing our Truth ~ no one listened in the first place.

The more you learn to love yourself, the less others are able to control your life by triggering old fears and insecurities. Love of self is empowering. Love of self attracts love and respect from others in all aspects of life. Giving love to others is easy. Giving love to ourselves and even receiving love from others is harder when there are no patterns established in our neural networks for doing so. This will require constant vigilance of our self-talk, monitoring of our thoughts that are self-deprecating and practicing giving ourselves affirmations of our worthiness and love-ability. Reprograming our brain/mind after years of telling ourselves we are not good or not good enough, will take time. Your ego will tell you that you're kidding yourself. Remember it doesn't want to change. You are inspired by your Higher Self to acknowledge yourself as a loveable person.

The model in Western society for Love has, for two thousand years, been the feminine face of God, Mother Mary. Her Love is considered ideal, unconditional and healing. We can give ourselves this same Love by focusing on our worth as a child of Father/Mother God. We can welcome ourselves Home as prodigal daughters of the Goddess.

WHAT I LOVE ABOUT ME

- I RESPECT MY ELDERS.
- I TREAT OTHERS WITH KINDNESS.
- I LOVE ANIMALS.
- I HAVE A GOOD SENSE OF HUMOR.
- I HAVE A BEAUTIFUL SMILE.

Make a list of all the things you love about yourself. Here are some ideas. If you have difficulty thinking of things you like, think of things you admire in friends or associates. You cannot see qualities in others that you do not have in yourself. So don't hesitate to name values that you would like to nurture in yourself. You are learning to express appreciation for yourself. No one in our society has been encouraged to do this. In fact, we have been discouraged from doing this! That stems from an old Puritan ethic that sparing the rod spoils the child. What nonsense! The Truth is loving ourselves leads to success in all facets of our lives.

I NOW AFFIRM MY SELF-ESTEEM

I now give myself loving messages,
acknowledging the Truth of who I Am.
If I learned from others,
either deliberately or inadvertently,
that I was not good or not good enough,
all children of Father-Mother God
are made in God's image, and
are, therefore, infinitely loveable.

THE TEMPLE OF LOVE

You are escorted into the Etheric Temple of the Goddess. You see beside you a Divine Being. You recognize Mother Mary, your Guardian Angel or another Being of Light that you know loves you and supports your Highest and Best. You stand in front of a pedestal that holds a Holy grail ~ a Sangrial. You see that it is filled with Holy Water. This water glows with the Pink Essence of Divine Love, Oneness and Reverence for All Life. You reach out and immerse your hands in the cool refreshing water. You feel the Spirit of Love penetrating your palms and fingers. It moves up your arms into your shoulders and across your torso, then fills your entire body with tingling rosy Light.

Your heart is filled with Love. From this Center of Love every cell of your body is filled with exquisite Light and feelings of Love and Gratitude for this Life. The Essence of Love awakens your Loving nature and reminds you that you too are a Goddess, a daughter of our Divine Mother God.

You bask in the sensations of Divine Love and Light, witnessing an aurora of crystalline pink, sapphire blue and sunshine yellow Light cascading around the Temple's columns, bathing Life on Earth and extending into the Heavens. This Light signifies the balance of Divine Love, Divine Power and Divine Wisdom.

All Life has awakened to Mother God's Love. With deep appreciation you thank your Divine Companion and return to your physical reality, bringing with you the multifaceted qualities of Love you have absorbed in the Temple of LOVE.

I AM EMBRACED BY THE ARMS OF MOTHER GOD'S CRYSTALLINE PINK LIGHT OF DIVINE LOVE.

I AM RESTORING MY LIFE TO ITS ORIGINAL BLUEPRINT

The fourth quality to appreciate is the purity at the center of every electron, atom, molecule and cell that comprises our bodies. Our model, the archetype for purity, is White Tara. She reminds us that we can witness the events taking place on Earth through our enhanced senses without having any negative energy reach the Purity of who we are at the core of our Being.

The immaculate concept is usually thought of in terms of the Catholic Church who proclaimed in 1854 that Mary, Mother of Jesus, must have been born free of original sin. The trouble with this idea is that the dogma of the church presumes that everyone else is contaminated by the original sin committed by Adam and Eve when they ate the fruit of the Tree of Knowledge of Good and Evil and were expelled from the Garden of Eden. Many of the stories told in the scriptures were first told orally to a population of illiterate people. In fact, there were no books available for the populus to read until the invention of the printing press in the 1454.

As we open our minds to more expansive views of our fall from Grace, we can begin to perceive the purity within each human being, no matter what outer appearances might suggest. The Essence of our Father-Mother God, like Holy DNA, resides within us. If we think of all human beings as made in the image of God, whatever the perception of God might be, then there is a spark of Divinity in each soul. That spark would contain the immaculate concept for the individual. We could think of that spark containing the blueprint for the life of each person. When we trust in the purity at the core of our being, we find the promise that whatever we have done, we are redeemable. We can always turn to the Divine within us.

Myths abound that promise restoration, renewal, resurrection and ascension. The great avatar Jesus said that we would be able to do all the things he did and more because we also had the ability to perform miracles. We were assured that by living a life of truth, service and love ~ love of God, others *and* self ~ that we would achieve the Kingdom of Heaven here on Earth.

Purity is a quality. You can buy a container of sugar or salt, for example, but you cannot buy a container of purity. From the purity within you, you can see the best within others in spite of outer appearances. The Goddesses, especially White Tara, Mother Mary, and Kuan Yin model for us the peaceful Presence of one who looks beyond surface behaviors and recognizes the beauty, the purity within. This vision sees through the external façade and into the heart of an adult's inner child who was wounded so deeply that she forgot her connection to the Divine.

Trauma can disconnect us from our Higher Selves, from our sense that we are children of the Creative Source, and have a spark of the Divine, like Cosmic DNA, in us. Trauma is inflicted by a perpetrator and the victim perceives herself as bad, wrong, or at fault. It would be very difficult to feel connected to the Divine in these circumstances.

If we believe that a Core of Purity resides within each cell of our being, it is possible to perceive the Core of Purity in the heart, mind and body of others. We could be led, as we connect so deeply with others, to the conclusion that we are all One. This perception of Oneness is a shift in consciousness from the typical view that we are separate. With this shift of consciousness we can see beyond the illusion to know that we are One with every other human being. We are one with the Earth and all life upon her including all plants, animals and minerals. We are One with the Elements: Earth, Air, Water and Fire. We are One with all of Creation.

These are BIG ideas. When I first began to question, through the lens of spirituality, I knew that I was a physical, mental, emotional *and* spiritual being. I believed from a knowing deep within me that there was a loving God and that when I passed from this life my Spirit would leave my physical body and enter Heaven, Nirvana, a transcendent realm. Near death reports consistently told of the spirit, the soul of a person, going through tunnels of light and entering heavenly realms before returning to life in a body. If my Spirit continued to exist after this life, it became easy to conceive of my Spirit as eternal, therefore, to have existed before this life.

In doing regressions I first experienced how my Spirit eagerly welcomed coming into a body ~ this body ~ and looked forward to life. What was surprising was how hard life was once I incarnated. In other regressions I experienced past lives, remembrances of lives I had never heard of or seen in any books or movies. I felt totally at peace and without judgement as I saw myself in different bodies, cultures, races, and genders. I witnessed myself committing acts I would never consider doing now. And I thought about the Law of the Circle. Would acts of harming others return to me in the future?

Believing in reincarnation is not essential to understanding how to improve the quality of this life. Everything we need to deal with is present here and now. I have found in my own life and in a counseling practice of over 30 years that a belief in a Higher Power and a commensurate belief in one's Higher or True Self is a great help in resolving trauma, finding forgiveness of self and others, and ultimately experiencing acceptance and peace of mind with what this life has presented.

Knowing, not just thinking, that a Core of Purity exists within you is a peace-promoting way to create a life of purpose and fulfillment.

THE WHITE LIGHT OF PURITY

I light a white candle on my altar
and gaze into its flame.
The flame is a symbol of purity.
I envision a flame of purity
blazing within every cell of my body.
I focus on *freedom* from any impurities
that could reside in each cell.
The flame of purity assures me that

I AM INFINITELY LOVED.

I AM FREE

I envision myself sitting in the middle of a large net. The cords of this net encircle me and extend from me to people and circumstances that have been problematic in the past. I now desire to have any cords that connect me to relationships or conditions that no longer serve me to be severed. I see that as I bring my attention to each person, place or thing, one at a time, a Being of Light with a mighty sword cuts me free. Each individual cord is cut and I am freed from discomfort, disharmony, or dis-ease of any kind. In turn, anyone or anything that has been bound to me and encumbered by ties that do not serve the Highest and Best for All Life is also FREE.

SHADOWS BE GONE

The core of every electron in my body is pure
and encoded with the Beauty and Truth of Who I AM.

Unconsciously, I have, throughout my lifetime,
misqualified my Life Energy in ways that have created shadows
that surround the perfect tiny electrons
that comprise my body and mind.

With humility and deep appreciation for the inherent perfection
of my body and mind, I now invoke
the White Flame of Purity to cleanse and purify
each electron, gently removing any shadows
that are cloaking the elemental substance of my being.
I see the shadows fading from sight
and the glow of perfection being restored
to every atom, molecule and cell of my body temple.

I AM VIBRANTLY HEALTHY

To heal on any level, whether it be physical, mental, emotional or spiritual, we need to consider both genetic and epigenetic factors. We have learned from cell biologist Bruce Lipton that our genes are not our destiny. That means that just because someone in our lineage had a particular disease, we are not destined to inherit it. On the other hand, we like to think that because an ancestor lived to be 100, we have the genes to do so as well. Science is revealing that going beyond the genes and considering epigenetic factors, those things in our environment and experience, play a much more significant role in our health and longevity than we thought.

One environmental influence that it is helpful to consider is the rise of the medical establishment over the last century. Larry Dossey, a physician who has served as an executive director of *The Journal of Science and Healing*, promotes alternative therapies. In *Reinventing Medicine: Beyond Mind-Body to a New Era of Healing*, Dr. Dossey introduced three eras of medicine. The first he described as Era I, which began around the turn of the last century. Doctors were beginning to provide care in hospitals and had two methods of delivering that care: pharmaceuticals, i.e., drugs, and surgery, the go-to options still depended upon today.

Era II began in the middle of the 1900s when mind and body were reunited after 400 years of separation that had been mandated by the Catholic Church. Spirit (considered the mind) was the province of the religious sector while the body could be addressed within the domain of physicians. During Era II, doctors began to observe that what individuals thought and felt impacted their health. Biofeedback equipment was demonstrating the connection between what was going on in the body and the body's relationship to what was going on in the mind.

Biofeedback therapy was then used to train patients to voluntarily control bodily functions such as their heart rates which had been thought to be strictly an involuntarily function. This reunification of mind and body suggests that Spirit is within each individual as well. Wayne Dyer has said that we are Spiritual Beings having a physical experience, not physical beings having a Spiritual experience.

Dr. Carl Simonton, a radiation oncologist, directed a clinic that treated cancer patients by teaching them relaxation and visualization techniques. Reports of cures using these unconventional treatments were questioned at the time, but mind-body healing continues to be observed today as people link their wellness to their positive thoughts and emotions. Recently a little boy with brain tumors was reported to have used imaginary missiles to blast the tumors away. When someone heals in this manner they don't talk about the disease being in remission, they talk about it as completely gone, and they are free from any fear that it might return.

Era III, according to Dossey, began at the beginning of the new millennium. During this new era non-local healing appears to be occurring. For example, a hospital patient's name could be given to a prayer group such as a group of Southern Baptists or a group of Tibetan monks. The patient, unknown to any members of the group, could then be prayed for. The religion or denomination of the group does not impact results. Although patients are not reported to experience instantaneous healing, they do take less medication and spend fewer days in the hospital. By projecting thoughts ~ prayers ~ of healing to an individual in a distant location (non-local), improvements in health and well-being are being achieved faster than anticipated.

Many people are beginning to think about health and the potential for healing outside the allopathic medical model. I have certainly appreciated that model when my husband had a stroke and needed medical diagnostics and treatments, and when he needed hip replacement surgery. Yet, I am also a proponent of alternative methods, especially those that focus on the individual's ability to look within to discover inner resources to help themselves.

This *inner vision* is essential for healing ourselves. In the ancient Mayan culture the Goddess Ixchel (pronounced *ee shell*) was called upon for Her Divine assistance especially to empower childbearing women. The qualities of the Divine Feminine are called forth by nurses, midwives and other caregivers in our modern society. Positive thinking that focuses on one's own ability to heal or the unshakable belief that Divine Intervention will heal a disease combine modern psychological concepts together with age-old spiritual beliefs. Cathedrals are strewn with crutches indicating that prayers to the Virgin Mary and the Divine Mother can yield miraculous results.

Dr. Gladys McGarey, a 103-year-old physician who was a dear friend and colleague, recently made her transition. Her teaching is legendary. She stated that "Love is what really does the healing." This medical doctor tells us Love *is* the healer. She calls upon the individual's *physician within*. During her long career she worked with her patients' inner resources to promote their health. It behooves us to love ourselves well (i.e. into health), and to love ourselves well enough to stay healthy all of our lives.

Peter McWilliams wrote "Our thoughts create our reality—not instantly, necessarily, as in "Poof! There it is"—but eventually. Where we put our focus—our inner and outer vision—is the direction we tend to go." McWilliams titled his 1988 book *You Can't Afford the Luxury of a Negative Thought*. Illness can result from negative thought patterns, habits of thought that build over time. He states: "Negative thinking helps provide the *opportunity*. The illness takes it from there." Our worry is the practice of habitually thinking negatively, thereby creating the very thing we are worrying about.

I learned years ago about worry, which focuses our energy on what we don't want, and all the negative words we use daily that sabotage our health. Saying "I *have* a disease" (you can substitute the name of any malady) attaches the condition to you. As I have said before, our brains are very literal. If you say you "have" a condition, your brain considers this a directive and will, over time, create it. To use your thinking positively in support of your health, begin to notice how you talk about your health ~ and then, begin to use more positive words and phrases like "I am vibrantly healthy. I am feeling better and better every day."

Caroline Myss, a medical intuitive, author and speaker, has written *Why People Don't Heal and How They Can* (1997). Myss notes the language we use to speak about our wounds, what she calls *woundology*! Because it yields lots of attention, sympathy and benefits in our society, we talk about our wounds all the time. Remember that what we think about, and tell ourselves, becomes our reality. If you are speaking the language of woundology, STOP now! Myss says that woundology "amounts to a kind of welfare state of the soul, paying people dividends for blithely refusing to better their condition." When we become addicted to our wounds and the payoff we get from telling everyone about them, we don't change, and our ego programming is reinforced.

One of the methods Myss recommends to heal ourselves involves calling upon our inner reserves of energy, what she calls our "cellular bank account." This process is aided by recognition of the Jungian notion that the collective unconscious, which is part of our own consciousness, holds images of archetypes. All of the Goddesses are original models ~ archetypes ~ of qualities within each of us.

We can view our Wounded Child as an archetype, symbolic of the difficulties we faced as children. Then, with love and respect for this Inner Child who survived traumatic events, we can nurture ourselves, embracing the Child in our imaginations with Love, Compassion, and Healing. These are the qualities of the Divine Feminine that have been modeled for us by the Goddesses and are those attributes that have lain dormant within us.

The brain does not know the difference between what is real and what is imagined! Explaining how this process works, Newberg and Waldman say in *Words Can Change Your Brain*:

> In the center of our brain there's a walnut-shaped structure called the thalamus. It relays sensory information about the outside world to the other parts of the brain. When we imagine something, this information is sent to the thalamus. Our research suggests that the thalamus treats these thoughts and fantasies in the same way it processes sounds, smells, tastes, images, and touch. And it doesn't distinguish between inner and outer realities. Thus, if you think you are safe, the rest of your brain assumes that you are safe. But if you ruminate on imaginary fears or self-doubt, your brain presumes that there may be a real threat in the outside world.

So if we use our imaginations to picture ourselves healing, comforting the child we used to be, it is possible we can actually heal the past!

Myss reminds her readers that their core beliefs may be perpetuating ill health. One such belief might be, "The only way I can get love is to be sick." If love and attention are only provided when we are ill, it would be hard to give up that belief. Reframing the notion to "This illness is showing me that it is time for me to change," invites us to perceive the malady as an opportunity for healing rather than another experience of fear that changing will prevent us from receiving the love we long for.

Creating a new vocabulary dedicated to your health is important. If you need to, write words and phrases on 3 x 5 cards and place them in pockets or purses that you can reach with ease. I write affirmations of health and well-being on sticky notes and place them on my bathroom mirror. I see them either directly or in my peripheral vision every time I comb my hair or brush my teeth.

When the impulse to talk about your wounds arises again, pull out a card with an affirmation of well-being. Decks of Goddess cards, Angel cards, and more are available for purchase. These cards often have inspiring messages to raise your spirits and shift your energy to more positive thoughts.

There are other words that trip us up all the time. *Try* is one of those words. Try is a failure word. When you hear someone say they have tried, you automatically think: *they tried but failed*. We use action words when we accomplish our goals: I passed the test, for example. Prior to taking a test, saying "I will *try* to pass the test" or "I *hope* I pass the test" uses words that have the connotation of doubt and dread. I heard so many fellow college students going in to take a test saying they hoped they passed the test. Did they study? If they prepared it is likely they would do well. If not, they would cling to the *hope* of passing. Replace the word *hope* with *trust*: "I *trust* I pass the test." There is promise and assurance in the word trust. And be sure to substitute the word *challenge* for the word *problem*. When you say challenge, it feels like you can overcome any obstacle rather than anticipating that the situation is unsolvable or insurmountable.

Dr. Gates, founder of the *SpectraDynamics* Program, said "More people are sick because they are unhappy than unhappy because they are sick." She noted that stress and tension contributed to unhappiness which leads to a repetitive cycle of negative thinking, negative emotions, and, subsequently, to some form of physical dis-ease. This could be anything from acne to arthritis, from headaches to heart attacks.

The mind-body connection is more and more apparent in creating our disorders and especially in healing those disorders. A technique that works well is *Focusing*, discovered by Professor Eugene Gendlin at the University of Chicago. He observed patients who were able to make positive changes in their lives. Focusing is a skill inherent in everyone. It is the ability to trust our bodies and access our feelings as those that we can rely upon to tell us what we need to change.

Like using archetypes, body imagery is used while *focusing* to identify a symbol or disfunction within your body that represents an emotion. When I learned the Focusing technique in graduate school, I was taught to become quiet and focus on a feeling, a bodily sensation. You might say, "This anger I feel inside seems like tightness in my chest." Utilizing the technique on your own, you would close your eyes and ask yourself what the discomfort looks like. You might visualize any tightness as a tightly wound spring, or a stainless steel knife. Look closely and identify its temperature, texture, color, weight and any other characteristics.

As you bring your attention to this sensation, your focused attention helps it shift. Usually we just want to make the sensation go away. Now, as it receives your attention, it responds. A sharp knife depicting pain might become a magic wand. If you ask yourself for something else within you that will help the discomfort transform, a sheath might appear to hold the weapon until it is ready to leave entirely. The tightly coiled spring might begin to uncoil forming ripples in a pool. As it unwinds you experience relief. The release signals the healing that is taking place. A woman I counseled found a buzz saw roiling in her stomach. As she described it, her focused attention precipitated a change, and it became a lotus blossom floating on a calm pond.

Using the power of your own consciousness, inner vision and wisdom you can begin to heal your distress or dis-ease. Small changes in the words you use, the way you talk to yourself, can create immediate changes for the better. As you appreciate medical assistance when needed but cultivate your own healing energies, you can increase your health, improve your longevity and build your Health Quotient. We may have just invented a new term: like IQ (Intelligence Quotient) and EQ (Emotional Quotient), it is HQ. This is your Health Quotient administered from your Headquarters (HQ - pun intended). In your brain/mind is the Wisdom to unite mind and body - psyche and soma - to find somatic remedies for any discomfort you are experiencing.

Dr. Herbert Benson, author of *The Relaxation Response*, told us fifty years ago:

> When your mind is quiet, when focusing has opened a door in your mind, visualize an outcome that is meaningful to you. If you are intent on alleviating a pain, envision yourself without the pain. If you are concerned with your performance at work or on the golf course or tennis court, imagine yourself performing well in these venues. Whatever your goal, these two steps can be powerful, allowing anyone to reap the benefits of the Relaxation Response and take advantage of a quiet mind to rewire thoughts and actions in desired directions.

In that spirit, you can write a letter to yourself affirming your health, optimum performance or success in any facet of your life. You can practice *Focusing* on bodily sensations to eliminate any discomfort. You can state affirmations that counter old thoughts and statements you have been repeating which have been negative or self-deprecating. You can begin to silence that critical voice within that is simply repeating old admonitions you heard as a child. Any and all of these activities will improve the quality of your health. Your prayers heal - so said Dr. Benson, Dr. Dossey and the high percentage of physicians who are reported to believe that prayers help a patient's recovery.

What you do with these practices is shift your mind from the belief that you have to have evidence to believe that something is true to a belief that believing is seeing. Psychologist and motivational speaker Wayne Dyer wrote a book on this subject: *You'll See It When You Believe It.*

A LETTER TO MYSELF

My letter to myself affirms that I Am vibrantly healthy.
I let go of phrases that reinforce
any discomfort, dis-ease or discord.

I write about my wholeness, worthiness and love-ability.
Not only am I able to give love, I now receive love
knowing that I AM a child of God,
worthy of my Father-Mother God's Love
for the unique expression of Life that I AM.

I choose my words wisely, expressing only my perfection,
for my brain/mind is an obedient servant
that will follow my instructions to the letter.

Therefore, I use words that out-picture
my Highest and Best.

It may feel like I am faking it,
but this is the path to making my Divine Qualities
my reality.

I fake it, until I make it!

**I AM RADIANTLY BEAUTIFUL.
I AM VIBRANTLY HEALTHY.
I AM ETERNALLY YOUTHFUL.
I AM PERFECT IN FORM AND FUNCTION.**

FOCUSING

I sit quietly, allowing myself to feel
any discomfort in my body.
When I find an uncomfortable sensation
I close my eyes
and focus on its location,
where I feel it in my body.

I describe that feeling by sensing its
Shape, Color, Temperature, Texture,
Visual Image and any other characteristics.

I focus on the image/sensation,
asking what it needs
to shift, relax or be more at ease.

As I pay attention,
I experience the transformation of my discomfort.

Symbolically, a knife may become a feather;
a hard stone may become a soft pillow;
a rusty saw blade may become
a lotus blossom
floating on a calm pond.

As uncomfortable sensations transform,
I feel whole, healthy and free.

**I AM IMMERSED IN THE EMERALD GREEN LIGHT
OF HEALING.**

I LIVE A GRACE-FILLED LIFE

The Three Graces, those lithe figures dancing with joy, are pictured in the Archetype section of this book. In Greek mythology the Three Graces are sister goddesses who symbolize the qualities of grace, beauty and charm. Aglaea is the name of the goddess exemplifying beauty or radiance; Euphrosyne embodies joy; and Thalia's name means bloom.

Venus, the Roman Goddess, also known as the Greek Goddess Aphrodite, symbolizes feminine grace, beauty and love. Her grace is portrayed in statues and paintings like the Venus de Milo in the Louvre. Representations of grace and beauty have existed for millennia, but generally women have not internalized those messages by acknowledging those qualities within themselves.

Alice Walker, author of *The Color Purple*, said this about a woman's tendency to shrug off compliments:

> If you say how lovely she is, or how beautiful her art is, or compliment anything else her soul took part in, inspired, or suffused, something in her mind says she is undeserving and you, the complementor, are an idiot for thinking such a thing to begin with. Rather than understand that the beauty of her soul shines through when she is being herself, the woman changes the subject and effectively snatches nourishment away from the soul-self, which thrives on being acknowledged.

Why women, even at young ages, deny their loveliness, their beauty, or their accomplishments is the result of cultural beliefs and practices that have impressed girls with the idea that they are not worthy. To rebel against cultural norms is futile. What works is learning to love ourselves. I just bought some new cosmetics. The written description of how to apply these products includes some advertising which states: "Discover the depth of your inner beauty." The passage ends with: "It's about inner self-love." This is a powerful message and is catching on. This company knows that women want to love themselves, even when it starts with using products that just work on the surface.

Self-awareness is essential to Loving ourselves. This consciousness is what many believe was the message conveyed two thousand years ago at the dawn of the Piscean Age. Now, in the Age of Aquarius, we can better understand the meaning of the greatest commandment. When asked which commandments were the greatest, the young rabbi responded:

> You shall love the Lord your God with all your heart, and with all your soul, and with all your mind. This is the greatest and first commandment. And the second is like it: You shall love your neighbor as yourself. (Mark 12: 21-31)

You don't awaken each morning planning what you will steal or whom you will kill. That is Old Testament thinking. We have, blessedly, in two thousand years, grown wiser than that. We do not have to be reminded not to steal or kill.

It is time to manifest the perfection within every human being ~ to love our neighbors while we love ourselves. The awakening of the Divine Feminine creates an appreciation for the faculties of the right brain, which have lain dormant for aeons of time. Now girls and women, as well as many men, everywhere are feeling the surge of the qualities of intuition, creativity, emotional expression, and imagination. Loving ourselves opens a door to receiving grace.

Grace is a gift beyond price. Grace is a gift from God. Moving through life with Grace means we know we are safe, we can trust the Universe to provide for us and, whatever happens, we are enfolded in a mantel of Divine energy that infinitely supports our Highest and Best.

Wikipedia says this about Grace:

> **Divine grace** is a theological term present in many religions. It has been defined as the divine influence which operates in humans to regenerate and sanctify, to inspire virtuous impulses, and to impart strength to endure trial and resist temptation; and as an individual virtue or excellence of divine origin.

In *The Next Step* Patricia Cota-Robles discusses grace in terms giving selfless service, what she calls *ministering grace*. "Selfless, giving service is the fastest, surest road to Spiritual development. It is not only the fastest, surest path but also the most fulfilling and rewarding." Receiving Grace seems like a miracle. Giving Grace is a free will choice that can be revitalizing for our hearts and minds.

Archetypes and metaphors use familiar terms and actions, particularly in painting and sculpture, to signify characteristics that are able to convey a quality or value. For hundreds of years people without the ability to read could understand in the stained glass windows of cathedrals, in the statues in temples, mosques and churches, and in art displayed on walls and ceilings of public buildings the unstated meanings: Divine Grace flows to us.

A Grace-full life is one that is filled with a sense of self-love and the knowledge that one's gifts are worthy of being shared. It is not wise to hide one's light under a bushel. As we will learn from Amaterasu, our Light is vital to life on Earth. This is not vanity. It is an acknowledgment of Universal Law. Our inner knowing is that gladly sharing one's treasures activates the Law of the Circle and abundance returns to us.

I AM BATHED IN THE RUBY LIGHT OF GOD'S GRACE.

THE GIFT OF GOD'S GRACE IS MINE

When I think of God's Grace,
I think of how I can grace the lives of others.
My experiences, knowledge and talents
are unique to me.
I offer them according to the Divine Plan for my Life.
I await the telepathic directions
I am able to receive
from my Higher Presence.

I FORGIVE MYSELF AND OTHERS

I have had a challenge with forgiveness. It always felt like I was letting the other guy ~ the offender ~ off the hook. In my studies of this delicate and complicated subject I have found a definition that at least feels right: *forgiveness is letting go of the desire to have had a different past ~ letting go of the desire for anything to be different than the way it showed up in my life.* Wanting a different past or a different outcome for a previous experience is futile. Accepting what happened can be hard, but it is possible. Holding onto grudges, resentments and hatred is truly self-defeating. Malachy McCourt (someone I had never heard of until I looked up this immortal quote) said resentment (that is, unforgiveness) is like taking poison and expecting the other person to die.

This whole concept of forgiveness is based on principles handed down to us over centuries. Old Testament texts tell us "an eye for an eye, a tooth for a tooth." Mahatma Gandhi commented that this philosophy would leave the whole world blind and toothless. The admonition suggests that punishment should be dealt out in the same manner in which the offense was committed. But it is not complete. This is only part of the Natural Law of the Circle. Good *and* bad, what we send out returns to us.

This is not a New Age thought. It is an age-old precept that if we express positive energy in thought, word, feeling or deed, positive energy returns to us. It's the New Testament teaching: *what we cast upon the waters comes back to us. We reap what we sow.* Everyone can understand the metaphor that if we plant tomatoes, we should not expect to harvest a different crop. *Like attracts like.*

Even the ancient Lord's Prayer tells us to forgive as we would be forgiven. We are asking God to forgive our trespasses in the same way in which we forgive others! I'd like better forgiveness than I have been able to mete out. Perhaps that means I am ready to change!

For aeons of time we have justified our judgments of others and our demands for retribution. This is not the New Testament notion of loving our enemies. Matthew 5:43-45 says, "You have heard that it was said, 'Love your neighbor and hate your enemy.' But I tell you, love your enemies and pray for those who persecute you, that you may be children of your Father in heaven." Now, that is a responsibility! Watch any news on television and you can see that most people are not doing this.

I have wondered "for *giving* what?" What are we giving? Perhaps it is the love that the Scriptures tells us goes beyond loving our friends. But loving our enemies? The Lord of the Old Testament said that vengeance was His and He would repay any wrongdoing. In the language of the illiterate people of the time, I think the scripture was saying that Natural Law (the Laws of Physics and of our Creative Source) will prevail. In time, any negativity will return to those who have transgressed against others. It's not our job to demand retribution. The Creator set it up for us to have the bread (the energy, positive or negative) we cast upon the waters (the vibrations we send out) come back to us. *Loving* stops the cycle of hurting each other.

Wayne Dyer, an amazingly insightful author and speaker, said, "Giving is the key to forgiving."

Keep in mind that it is impossible to create any bitterness or hatred toward others when your primary objective is to be a giving human being. Forgiveness comes almost automatically when you detach yourself from the need to get something and instead focus on reaching out to others. The irony is that the less you are obsessed with getting and the more willing you are to give, the more you seem to get.

Louise L. Hay, who founded Hay House Publishing, wrote in her book *You Can Heal Your Life* that forgiveness is a choice. She recommends repeating this mantra if we are *willing* to forgive someone, even when we don't know how:

"I forgive you for not being the way I wanted you to be.
I forgive you and I set you free."

Hay refers to the *Course in Miracles* saying, "that all dis-ease comes from a state of unforgiveness." If we are suffering from an illness we should be thinking about whom we need to forgive. It might be ourselves.

Dr. Dorothy Gates encouraged us to forgive our parents or other individuals who helped raise us by saying:

I forgive you for wanting to shape me in ways that suited you, but did not recognize or respect my individuality. I forgive your need to mold me into a preconceived pattern that may have frightened me or distorted my vision of myself. I honor my Higher Self and release old patterns of imperfection. I AM FREE.

Psychologists generally define forgiveness as "a conscious, deliberate decision to release feelings of resentment or vengeance toward a person or group who has harmed you, regardless of whether they actually deserve your forgiveness." However, it seems that we are somehow refusing to see a bigger picture ~ that we are still mired in the perception of being victims.

If the avatar of the last two thousand years told us to let our Light shine (Matthew 5:16), doesn't that imply that every child of God has Light within? If I focus on the Light, there is nothing to forgive. Behavior is NOT who we are or who anyone is. Colin Tipping wrote in *Radical Forgiveness*, when we have an issue with someone we should look for and see "*the Christ* [the Light] *in them.*"

Our task is to stop identifying with our wounded inner child and letting that child run our lives. Tipping calls this child "the whining little brat that lives in the back room of our mind, that unhappy victim who always can be relied upon to blame everyone else for our unhappiness." Ouch! Tipping's four-step process out of "*victimland*" is to first acknowledge that we created the situation as creators of our own reality. We are reminded to know that our Higher Selves are providing us with an opportunity to heal old underlying wounds. Second, is to notice our own judgments and love ourselves anyway. Accepting our humanity leads to a quick shift in our energy. Third, even though we have not been able to see the perfection or the bigger picture in this situation, we acknowledge our willingness to see that there is a Divine Plan at work. And fourth, we "choose the power of peace" to bring harmony, peace of mind and resolution to our lives. With patience and perseverance, this process is a Godsend.

What I have been learning is that we were imprinted with feelings of betrayal, abandonment, rejection or other atrocity when we were little. Our egos formed an identity around that imprint and figured out a way to survive then, and now, in similar situations, when we are triggered and feel again what we once felt, we go to our default response ~ fight, flight or freeze ~ and react the same way we did as a child. The process that worked the first time becomes a pattern of thinking, feeling and behaving that does not want to change. Why, our programmed ego minds ask, change something that worked?

But the strategies of a child no longer serve an adult. Most of the judgments we espouse were learned when we were children. As I have recognized my judgments, I have discovered them *not* to be mine at all. My own therapist, Sanjay Manchanda, has guided me to say, "Not me, not mine." I learned lots about judgment and blame in my family of origin. It was likely my parents learned to judge others in the homes of their parents as well. We think we can feel better when we are not responsible for transgressions ~ that someone else is to blame. This line of thinking leads to more blaming and a very dissatisfying life. It's difficult to take credit for doing good things while denying any accountability for things that appear bad or like failures. What I have come to realize is that my parents did the best they could do given the wisdom and experience they had at the time. I had this epiphany several decades ago so forgiving my parents was not even necessary. There was nothing to forgive.

I'll make another suggestion here as we consider the forgiveness, compassion and mercy of the Goddess Kuan Yin. She is still worshipped in the Far East and is a model for us to emulate. There is a story circulating on the internet that describes the practice of Ho'oponopono. This is an Hawaiian practice of reconciliation and forgiveness. It is said a doctor cured everyone in a mental health facility in Hawaii without ever seeing a patient! He held each person's file and repeated:

**I'm sorry. Please forgive me.
Thank you. I love you.**

I have used this practice over the years by naming someone with whom I was having difficulties and repeating this phrase during my prayer and meditation time. Sometimes I simply have not known what the issue was, but something was wrong. So I sincerely apologized for what the other person perceived I did wrong. Maybe I was just not aware of how the individual was harmed on my watch. I truly regret that. I asked for forgiveness. I expressed my gratitude and I told them in my visualization that I loved them. My experience is that hearts soften, attitudes moderate and behaviors improve. It takes time, but it works.

I love science and psychology but I am dedicated to spirituality. So I call upon all of these tools and belief systems to improve the quality of our lives. And I believe that we all should have choices. One option might work for one person while another might be better for someone else.

One last story about forgiveness: a few years ago my husband and I attended a retreat. The man we all wanted to hear speak was a Rinpoche ~ a Holy man, a "precious one" ~ from Tibet. He spoke with the assistance of an interpreter. We asked him to tell us his story because we knew he had been harmed in some way and had a lesson in forgiveness to share. We wanted to know how he, as a Buddhist, forgave his persecutors. In the West we are still, much to my dismay, dealing with the incomplete eye-for-an-eye philosophy.

The Rinpoche sat on a dais we improvised for him. We all sat on the floor looking up at this kind man. He had walked in with a limp and showed some signs of disability as he folded his legs in a yogic lotus position. He told us that a few years ago he had spoken with the Dalai Lama in India and was told he needed to go back to Tibet. As an obedient disciple, he agreed. When he returned to Tibet he was arrested and jailed by the Chinese. For three years he was tortured until he escaped. On his journey to the United States he hurt his leg. In a New York hospital he was told his leg had become gangrenous and had to be amputated. He refused the surgery saying that he would use his own prayer and meditation practices to heal himself, and he did.

How did he forgive his captors? First, he said that torturing people was just their job. They did not know any better. This was the way they supported their families. Next, he said that, as a Buddhist, he must have done something to them in a past life for them to be torturing him in this life. Finally, and most powerfully, he said that they did not understand what they were doing in the context of reincarnation. They would have returned to them the harm they did to others in their next life. He put his head down and wept.

It took me two years of meditating to understand what he meant. This is the same declaration that Jesus made from the cross when he said "Father, forgive them, they know not what they do." When one believes in reincarnation, they know that in the next life, if not in this one, they will receive the same energy they expressed. According to this belief, the Chinese captors would experience great pain and suffering in a future life and our Beloved Rinpoche wept for them. That's true forgiveness.

I FORGIVE MYSELF

Today, this moment, I realize that I have been operating out of old programs inadvertently or deliberately instilled in me as I was growing up.
Many of these programs appear *not*
to serve my Highest Good.

I accept my vulnerability and my desire to please others, to conform, to fit into a family or societal structure that may not have been in my best interests. I know better now and
I choose to live in the Truth of who I AM.

I forgive myself for the mistakes I have made in the past and I step into a way of Being that honors my Highest Self.

I have a Code of Ethics that honors others and I behave in a manner that respects myself and all those with whom I interact.

I LET GO OF FEAR & UNRAVEL THE PAST

I have thought that if I let go, I will fall, I will die.
I would have to let go of my basic principles.
This *thing* should not have happened!
But I cannot undo it. How can I change the past?

The past is a tapestry woven with perishable thread.
I have woven knots into my fabric.
I now pluck them out. I envision whole cloth.

I repeat, "I forgive." I let go of any imperfection
in the fabric of my life.
The knots, made of fibers of thought and feeling,
are wafted away to be transmuted back into Light.

I let go. My Higher Self will catch me. She says,
"I will always hold you as you weave new patterns
into the fabric of your life. Soon you will know we are One
and your tapestry will be free of any imperfections."

The young woman pictured here could be any nationality. All cultures pray, forgive and ask for forgiveness.

I FORGIVE

Forgiving is FOR GIVING. In the ancient prayer we ask God to forgive us as we forgive others. This potent phrase tells us that while, at the same time as and in the same manner in which we forgive others, we would like God to forgive us.

If we withhold forgiveness, if we seek vengeance or have an attitude of resentment, we are asking the Divine to treat us the same way. Our prayers conform to Natural Law, in this case the Law of the Circle, therefore, we will receive the same kind of judgement, intolerance, vengeance or lack of love that we give out. This is not God punishing us, but ourselves acting in concert with Natural Law.

I give away my Best so it will come back to me with my
Love and Forgiveness magnified.

FORGIVENESS IS FREEDOM

As St. John said, forgiveness is the key to our prison cell
and we hold that key in our own hand.

Envision a key opening the lock on a door to a cell
(pun intended) in which you have been imprisoned.

Feel the freedom, the joy and the lightness as you breathe easier
and release the thoughts and emotions
that have held you captive.

YOU ARE FREE!

I AM SURROUNDED BY THE VIOLET LIGHT OF MERCY, COMPASSION AND FORGIVENESS.

I CAN SEE CLEARLY NOW

It seems that we are beginning to see with new eyes and hear with new ears. This ancient proverb suggests that one day we will awaken and see things in a new Light and hear things beyond what our sense of hearing formerly conveyed. Our minds will be opened to see a bigger picture, to behold others and their behaviors in a more compassionate and understanding manner. We will then affirm that, like Amaterasu, we see with Clarity, Divine Perception and Discernment.

The example that the legend of Amaterasu provides is that she awakened to the fact that life on Earth was imperiled without her Light in it. That's the message for you to absorb. Your Light is so valuable on this planet that without it all life is incomplete. With Clarity and Discernment you now perceive your own value. You *see* how your Life is essential to the Oneness of All Life. This is not egotism! It is a profound knowing that all life is valuable, so your Life must be too.

Let's look at Light and how it behaves. According to the Britannica online definition, "Light is an electromagnetic radiation that can be detected by the human eye." Light is not just visible to our eyes. Light is detectable on a spectrum which includes ultraviolet and infrared light. So we can open our minds to the possibility that Light ~ Life Energy ~ flows to us on each breath we take. Indeed, we all breathe the air that surrounds this planet, exchanging the oxygen, nitrogen and the gases that comprise this gossamer net of energy which we cannot see, but rely upon for our very lives.

Over two hundred years ago scientists wanted to know whether light was a particle or a wave. *Imperial News* of Imperial College London reported in April 2023 that:

The original double-slit experiment, performed in 1801 by Thomas Young at the Royal Institution, showed that light acts as a wave. Further experiments, however, showed that light actually behaves as both a wave and as particles – revealing its quantum nature.

Life cannot exist on this planet without Light. What is most interesting for us is that Light responds to our thoughts: if we expect it to behave as a particle, it does; if we expect it to behave as a wave, it does that. Light responds to how the scientists set up the experiment.

Our lives are experiments as well. How do we qualify the Light that we receive with each Breath? In the Far East the breath "provides the body's supply of life-energy (Sanskrit *prana*, Chinese *chi*, Japanese *ki*, Tibetan *thig-le* or *rlung*." This *is* our Life Energy. What do we do with it? Do we assimilate it into our bodies and project it out into the world infused with loving thoughts and positive feelings? Or do we misqualify that Light with fearful thoughts and negative feelings? It's up to us.

We have been considering the words we use as well as the energy we assimilate with each breath. Both the breath we inhale and the words we speak when we exhale (we cannot utter words on the inhalation) pass through our throats. This is a power center in our bodies. The first command spoken, according to Holy Scriptures, was "Let there be Light." Words are creative. Whatever you say through the language you use is an expression of what you believe. Therefore, you qualify your Life Energy with your ideas, your thoughts, your beliefs. These beliefs are true for you, but not necessarily true for others who have different ideas, thoughts and beliefs. Differences can be good. It is our judgements, our prejudices and the way we discriminate against others that do harm.

Everyone on this Earth is unique. The passage of Light and Breath through us is our privilege and responsibility to share with humanity as best we can. The Goddess Amaterasu discovered that her Light was so powerful that when she hid it all life suffered. I encourage you to know in your heart and mind that your Light is as valuable as the Goddess of the Sun demonstrated for us.

There's more. We can explore both ancient and modern texts to discover that we are more than our physical bodies. In awakening to the eternality of our Spirits, we *see* that this body is just the car that we drive throughout this life. Ironically, we treat it like a car. We take it for checkups, we repair body parts, and actually replace some parts when they are used up or broken.

Years ago I heard Gordon Graham, the author of *The One-eyed Man Is King*, speak. I will never forget what he said: "We have to fix our bicycles while we're riding them." In this metaphor, our bodies are like a bicycle, rather than a car. Life goes on. We have to make adjustments, change our programming, and learn to live in harmony with others while we engage in daily life. The world does not stop for us to catch up.

We have more than a physical body; we have an emotional, mental and etheric body as well. Around us is an invisible aura, an energy body known as our etheric body. We know with the advent of Kirlian photography that there is an energy field that extends a little beyond the physical body which can be seen with the proper equipment.

Every thought, feeling, and word we express passes through this energy field. It is said that this field is comprised of sensitive chemical ethers and it records all of the thoughts and feelings that we send forth. In this interpretation, our thoughts and feelings are themselves electromagnetic energy which we emanate and which returns to us in accordance with the Law of the Circle. When we see clearly how the Universe works, we can understand the importance of making sure that all of our transmissions ~ thoughts, words and feelings ~ are positive. That's the energy we would like to get back, so we can now be more careful about what we are sending out. The Law of Attraction and Scriptures have been telling us this for centuries.

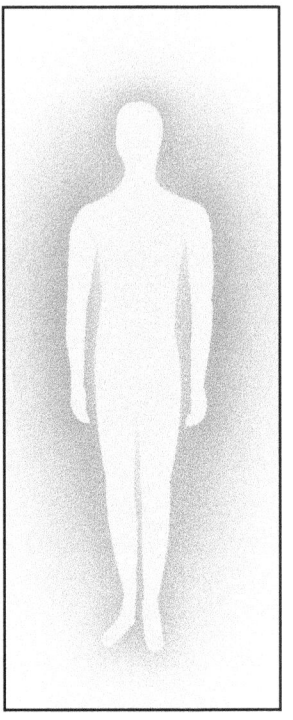

Remember that every child forms an identity, a self-image, by the way she is treated. If that treatment is negligent or abusive the child thinks she is to blame, at fault and unworthy of love or kinder treatment. In the child's eyes adults are all-knowing so if she is maltreated, there must be something wrong with her. All the treatment, all the impressions, all the hurts and kindnesses are recorded in her etheric body.

When we react to events in adverse ways, we are responding from identifying with our inner child who received similar treatment much earlier in life. A beloved teacher of mine, Barbara Findeisen, used to say: "Don't take your wounded child to the bank to ask for a loan. Leave her in the car and promise her an ice cream cone when you return. Go into the bank as your *wise adult* to negotiate your loan."

Every cell and organ within our physical body has an aura as well. This aura can surround each cell with a cloud of negativity or a halo of illumination. Our perceptions, opinions and choices form our ego. Regrettably, the ego likes to be right about everything, especially about our opinion of ourselves which forms early; so we hide our Light, or we behave in ways that confirm our subconscious beliefs. When opportunity knocks, when love shows up, we don't believe we are worthy of it, so we sabotage our own success and happiness.

Next, we have a mental body, an invisible energetic body that surrounds our physical and etheric bodies. Acknowledging this energetic field around us helps us understand that our thoughts extend beyond our physical brains and bodies. This is the mind as we understand it. The mental body interpenetrates all the other bodies and is responsive to the focus of our attention. Our attention is the entryway to our minds, indeed, to our consciousness. Our attention is focused through the lens of each sense, our data-gathering faculties of sight, smell, hearing, taste, touch, as well as our intuition and imagination. Our mental bodies ~ or minds ~ are full of images we have recorded throughout our lifetimes. Many of these are distortions, negativity that clutters our mind and keeps us mired in the past. Letting go of this excess and undesirable baggage is possible and exercises at the end of this section can facilitate that *letting go.*

It is important to remember that we have levels of consciousness that we think of as our multifaceted mind. Studies of our brain wave states over decades have shown that we have, in addition to a mental body and a physical brain structure, a subconscious mind holding implicit thoughts, a conscious mind capable of expressing explicit thoughts, and a superconscious mind that is connected to our True or Higher Selves. Meditation and prayer are portals to this greater awareness. Paradoxically, it is quieting the mind that leads to enhanced awareness and Divine Perception.

Our largest invisible energetic body is our emotional body. It encompasses our other bodies and is our feeling world. We learn to feel from the very beginning of our lives even as we develop in utero. Every cell, from the moment of our conceptions, records our perceptions of what is happening. Mother's feelings are interpreted as what is normal to feel in our limited experience in the womb. Is her world happy, safe, loving and stress-free, or is it filled with worry, fear and tension? All her thoughts and feel-

171

ings inculcate the cells of the precious child she carries. What a responsibility! As we open our eyes to see that each mother ~ and father ~ are vulnerable beings who are literally creating the next generation of human beings, we can treat them with compassion and love to insure that the children of the future are conceived, gestated and born in an atmosphere of love.

Our four lower bodies ~ physical, etheric, mental and emotional ~ are the expressions of the Creative Source on Earth. The essence of the Divine resides within us, *and* we have free will to express the Divinity within us ~ or not! Our egos implement our free will and direct our creative thoughts and feelings in ways that protect whatever it learned from our conception forward. It does not want to surrender to the Will of our Higher Selves. So it will keep doing what it has always done until we take charge of our lives and call upon our Divine qualities to create better lives.

It is almost counterintuitive to consider that what we are doing, those actions that seem to insure our survival, could be modified to bring us love, happiness, joy, prosperity and all of the Divine attributes, tangible and intangible. Yet, we cannot keep doing what we have always done if we want the world to reward us (reflect to us) instead of seeming to persecute us. This is victim consciousness! We cannot achieve our fondest wishes by insisting that the people and circumstances in the world change. The mirror of life reflects what we think and feel at deeply subconscious levels, so it is our job to change our thoughts and feelings from those of fear to those of love. That task is a process, not just a goal, and is the path to happier more abundant lives.

In pursuit of happier lives ~ as girls, as women ~ we can call upon our Divine Feminine Natures. We have archetypes who have modeled those qualities for centuries. We have an inner knowing that if the Divine exists within even one of us, it must exist within all of us. We can begin by trusting that this is true.

Margaret Starbird wrote *The Goddess in the Gospels*, a book that celebrates the Divine Feminine. As a devout Catholic she searched through scriptures and historical records to find evidence of the feminine face of God. She found the "bride" in the Old Testament *Song of Songs* and discovered that to the early Christians the Goddess in the Gospels was Mary Magdalene, the bride of Jesus. Images of the Virgin, Mother Mary, holding her child that were rendered by the early Christians were modeled on ancient images of Isis, the Egyptian goddess who was the sister/bride of Osiris and mother of Horus, regarded as the God of Light.

For over two thousand years the early reverence for the Divine Feminine has been distorted and disparaged. Women in the Western world have become accustomed to being regarded as subservient to men. We have been taught that a masculine God, the Father, created His children without a Mother. What a tragic misunderstanding!

We can see clearly now that the Feminine Face of God is all women. She is Us. We can, with authority, say: *I Am the Divine Feminine in a human body*. Marianne Williamson notes that "the woman who is truly self-aware knows that her self is a light from beyond this world, a spiritual essence that has nothing to do with the physical world."

To achieve this clarity can take some re-envisioning. It can help to kindle new awareness by engaging in therapy. Bibliotherapy, reading books, or video therapy, watching movies, can be self-therapy. Watch movies that are fun and enlightening. *On a Clear Day You Can See Forever* is a 1970s movie starring Barbra Streisand. It's a fantasy about a woman who seeks help from a psychiatrist. He falls in love with her, but how they end up together is quite a surprise. A more recent movie (2013) is *Now You See Me* in which illusionists mesmerize audiences. It's an entertaining mystery.

In *Healing and Regeneration through Color* author Corinne Heline alluded to color therapy:

> Light, color and beauty are to be key-words to New Age living. The Aquarian Age is essentially and primarily a color age. Lighter and higher tones of the spectrum are coming into visibility as, on the one hand, the atmosphere becomes clearer and more attenuated and the ethers more discernable; and, on the other hand, man's sense perception becomes more highly sensitized. With such changes in man and his environment we may expect to lay hold of hitherto undreamed-of powers linked to color radiations. New and amazing developments in the psychology and therapeutics of color are nearing application and public use.

365 Goddess is a daily guide book that has wonderful ideas to remind us of Goddess qualities and how we can connect with them. To allow the energy of Amaterasu into our homes, all we need to do is open the curtains wide and let the sun shine in! Author of this enchanting book, Patricia Telesco, encourages us:

> Once the curtains are opened, take a hand mirror and reflect the light into every corner of your home. This draws Amaterasu's unifying energy into your living space and guards against discord among all who dwell therein. Also, to ensure that no malevolence enters from outside the home, put a mirror facing outward in an eastern window (where Amaterasu rises). This is a Buddhist custom for turning away negativity and evil influences.

Music: Physician for Times to Come tells us that music is a "timeless therapy." Singing is a great help in creating a better mood, and lifting our spirits. Celebrate seeing clearly with song. Here are two of my favorites!

ON A CLEAR DAY YOU CAN SEE FOREVER
By Burton Lane and Alan Jay Lerner

On a clear day rise and look around you
and you'll see who you are.

On a clear day how it will astound you
that the glow of your being outshines every star.
You'll feel part of every mountain, sea and shore.
You can hear from far and near
A world you've never heard before.

And on a clear day, on a clear day,
you can see forever, and ever
and ever more.

I CAN SEE CLEARLY NOW
By Johnny Nash

I can see clearly now, the rain is gone.
I can see all the obstacles in my way.
Gone are the dark clouds that had me blind.
It's gonna be a bright, bright sun-shiny day.

I think I can make it now, the pain is gone.
All of the bad feelings have disappeared.
Here is the rainbow I've been prayin' for.
It's gonna be a bright, bright, sun-shinny day.

Look all around, there's nothin' but blue skies.
Look straight ahead, nothin' but blue skies.

I can see clearly now, the rain is gone.
I can see all the obstacles in my way.
Gone are the dark clouds that had me blind.
It's gonna be a bright, bright sun-shinny day.
It's gonna be a bright, bright sun-shinny day.

I SEE BEYOND OUTER APPEARANCES.

I SEE THAT SOMEONE WHO OFFENDS ME
IS A WOUNDED CHILD, UNABLE TO PERCEIVE
HIS OR HER OWN PERFECTION.

I NOW SEE WITH THE EYES OF A LOVING GODDESS.

I LET GO OF JUDGEMENTS AND LOOK FOR
THE BEST IN OTHERS, AND MYSELF.

I EMBRACE PARADOX.

I SEE THAT LIFE PRESENTS MANY CONTRACICTIONS.
I REALIZE THAT I AM AN INDIVIDUAL
AND I AM ALSO PART OF A GREATER WHOLE.

AS WAYNE DYER SAID:
"INDIVIDUALISM AND A SENSE OF WHOLENESS
ONLY APPEAR TO BE MUTUALLY EXCLUSIVE.
LIVING WITH THE PARADOX AND UNDERSTANDING
THAT TWO SEEMING OPPOSITES ALWAYS FUNCTION
WITHIN A HARMONIOUS WHOLE IS INTEGRAL TO
ENLIGHTENMENT."

I TRUST LIFE TO REFLECT MY WORTH
AT THE SAME TIME I SEE AND RESPECT
THE INHERENT WORTH OF OTHERS.

I AM A CRYSTALLINE BEING OF LIGHT.

LIKE A MIGHTY PRISM, I REFRACT
THE DIVINE LIGHT FLOWING THROUGH ME
AND RADIATE THAT LIGHT IN A MYRIAD OF COLORS
OUT INTO THE WORLD.

I AM ENFOLDED IN THE AQUAMARINE LIGHT
OF CLARITY AND DIVINE PERCEPTION.

I AM BALANCED & HARMONIOUS

What does it mean to be balanced? In the manner in which I am discussing the topic, it means to be equally aware of body, mind and spirit. It means to have left brain masculine abilities of logic, linguistics and analysis integrated with right brain feminine creative, artistic and intuitive abilities. It means to call upon both brain and heart to evaluate situations and make decisions.

The scales of justice represent balance. They symbolize weighing all evidence impartially so that each party in any legal dispute is treated fairly. The scales of justice are often associated with Lady Justice, a female figure who holds the scales in one hand and a sword in the other. The sword represents the authority of the law and the power to punish injustice.

Lady Justice is often depicted wearing a blindfold. The notion that justice is blind suggests that to be just means letting go of any prejudices, biases or beliefs that could influence fair and equal judgment. "Lady Justice is based on the Greek goddess Themis – honored as clear-sighted – and the Roman goddess Justicia – honored as representing the virtue of justice."

Balance is often paired with harmony, a word derived from the Greek "harmos" which means to fit together, to join or connect. What is of most interest here is developing the quality of harmony within, to unite masculine and feminine qualities that lead to an inner calm. When we are agitated or stressed we fall back on old ingrained habit patterns that keep us reacting to circumstances instead of accessing our inner *harmony*, our sense of tranquility, when we need it most.

When we are harmonious, we are self-assured and confident. An harmonious person is, according to my internet search:

Someone who embodies a sense of balance, peace, and overall well-being in their life and interactions with others. This individual typically maintains a sense of inner peace and calm, and they often seek to foster positive and constructive relationships with those around them.

When we are bringing our brains into balance and harmony we are reconciling the masculine and feminine attributes within our two cerebral hemispheres. Ideally, we are also balancing our mental activity, our thoughts, and our emotional activity, our feelings and our physical sensations. This includes the flow of hormones which connect our physical bodies to our mental and emotional bodies. We are self-regulating, a term that has become a buzz word in the realm of psychology.

Self-regulation is self-control. The theory suggests that we make choices regarding how to express our thoughts, emotions and behavior. Andrea Bell is quoted on the Positive Psychology website:

Someone who has good emotional self-regulation has the ability to keep their emotions in check. They can resist impulsive behaviors that might worsen their situation, and they can cheer themselves up when they're feeling down. They have a flexible range of emotional and behavioral responses that are well-matched to the demands of their environment.

Are we choosing our responses, or are we acquiescing to our conditioning and expressing our thoughts and feelings according to old programs? Becoming self-regulated means balancing and harmonizing our mental, emotional and physical selves so we are, indeed, choosing what we say and do. We often create problems for ourselves and others when we react from unconscious programming and forget to check in with our Higher Selves.

Harmony is not a word I hear used much in terms of finding inner peace. It is more often used in the realm of music. When two voices harmonize, they maintain their individual uniqueness but blend with each other in ways that enhance each voice as well as the song they are singing. We can begin to appreciate the quality of harmony both internally and externally like singers who create sounds that one could not achieve without the other.

Think of your body as an magnificent orchestra. Each organ, gland, tissue and cell is an instrument that responds to the conductor ~ you. As you think harmonious thoughts and express positive feelings, your body/orchestra creates beautiful music ~ health and wellbeing are yours. In this metaphor, you realize that dis-cord, dis-ease and dis-harmony in your thoughts and feelings create cacophony and dissonance within your body and mind.

I AM THE CONDUCTOR OF THE SYMPHONY OF MY LIFE

I AM the conductor of a magnificent orchestra.
Every instrument plays a perfect part
in the symphony of my life.

I see each precious member of this orchestra
playing beautiful melodies.

As I conduct this grand symphony, Harmony reigns.

The tones synchronize and each strain expresses its unique
vibration while it harmonizes with all the others.

I confidently conduct this symphony with reverence for my
Life and the Harmony that I can cocreate in the world.

In addition to the Harmony I now recognize is essential to the well-being of my physical, mental and emotional bodies, I see that my Spiritual Body also requires my recognition and appreciation. *Ask and ye shall receive* is a well-known proverb that suggests help from the Divine comes when we ask for it. We have free will which cannot be infringed upon, therefore, we must ask for assistance, according to this scriptural admonition. We ask our Higher Selves, that part of us that is our connection to our Creative Source, to God.

Respected author, speaker and physician Deepak Chopra merges ancient wisdom and quantum science to define our Higher Self:

> According to the discoveries of quantum physics, the body is actually a swirling mass of constantly changing energy. It has more in common with what we think of as "spirit" than what we think of as matter. It is the "you" behind all of the defenses and images you have created for yourself ... the you that really knows why you are here, what it is you need and how you can get it.

Dr. Chopra says, "By transcending to your personal core, the higher self, you discover your true nature—a blissful self of infinite worth."

Higher Self Yoga tells us our Higher Self is "our greatest potential."

> The Higher Self is the wise being within all of us. It is a calm, loving, and spiritual guide that brings our positive characteristics to the surface and tasks us with questioning our lower nature. When we live in alignment with the inner wisdom of our Higher Selves, we become the best possible version of ourselves. Our Higher Self knows our true purpose, and

encompasses our potential to live a fulfilling and joyous life through personal growth and self-awareness.

In *Your Sacred Self*, Wayne Dyer says, "There dwells within all human beings a divine energy. The power of this energy permeates our entire being and permits us to perform every function in the vast repertoire of human thoughts and behaviors. . . . Awaken this dormant energy."

As we recognize this divine energy ~ this Higher Self ~ we become more balanced. As we balance our physical, mental, and emotional bodies we naturally open to experiencing our Higher Self, our True Self, our God Self or our I AM Presence. This aspect of ourselves knows our innate worthiness. Our True Self is sometimes described as the *still small voice* that whispers to us. It provides guidance and assurance. It may seem that the wisdom we hear counters the typical responses we might have in any given situation. That is a key to recognizing that this voice is your quiet partner in making the best decisions, not the voice of ego who wants you to keep doing what you have always done, usually in anger, fear or resistance of some sort.

Telesco, in *365 Goddess*, reminds you to "balance your karmic checkbook."

We have a joke in our family about listening to our inner wisdom, that is, our Higher Selves. Our daughter was driving in Tucson one day and had a thought (a telepathic thought that sometimes speaks through our minds ~ that still small voice) that she should *not* take Grant Road. She dismissed this idea and took Grant Road anyway. There was construction on this street and it took much longer to reach her destination than it would have if she had taken an alternate route. Now when we find ourselves making choices that would benefit from our Higher Self's input, we just say: "Don't take Grant Road!"

I have observed that many people think that becoming *spiritual* has to be hard or that a spiritual life requires making sacrifices and practicing long hours of prayer or meditation. The Zen expression to *chop wood and carry water* suggests that every activity is a spiritual act. Everything we do ~ washing dishes, doing the laundry, preparing a meal, caring for our children, running errands, paying bills, doing our jobs ~ when done with joy and enthusiasm are all spiritual acts. This attitude conveys to the Divine that we appreciate this Life and all facets of it are opportunities to thank God and be in our Bliss.

Joseph Campbell is renowned for his remark, "Follow your bliss." Your *bliss* is your calling, the urge you have to live your life joyfully:

> Follow your bliss. If you do follow your bliss, you put yourself on a kind of track that has been there all the while waiting for you, and the life you ought to be living is the one you are living. When you can see that, you begin to meet people who are in the field of your bliss, and they open the doors to you. I say, follow your bliss and don't be afraid, and doors will open where you didn't know they were going to be. If you follow your bliss, doors will open for you that wouldn't have opened for anyone else.

Following our bliss can start by being in balance and harmony in the present moment, performing the most menial tasks. Abraham Lincoln said, "Most folks are as happy as they make up their minds to be."

Start now. Make up your mind to be happy now. Don't wait. Every task you perform is an opportunity to be happy or to be sad and resentful. Start by feeling blissful now. What could be more spiritual, more harmonious than that?

I AM ENVELOPED IN THE MAGENTA LIGHT OF
HARMONY AND BALANCE.

I MOVE WITH BALANCE AND EASE.

I TAKE A FEW MINUTES EACH DAY
TO WALK IN A FIGURE 8 PATTERN.
PERFORMING THE "INFINITY WALK" IS
MINDFUL WALKING.

MY MOVEMENTS ARE LIGHT, GRACEFUL AND
COORDINATED.

I AM A CELL IN THE BODY OF HUMANITY.

I AM A CELL IN THE BODY OF THE UNIVERSE.

I AM A CELL IN THE BODY OF ALL CREATION.

THE HEALTH OF HUMANITY,
THE HEALTH OF THE UNIVERSE AND
THE HEALTH OF CREATION

~ ALL EXPRESSIONS OF THE CREATIVE SOURCE ~

DEPEND ON HARMONY WITHIN EACH CELL.

I AM AN HARMONIOUS CELL IN THE BODY OF
ALL CREATION.

FRAGRANT FLOWER ESSENCES

"Flower essences are liquid, pattern infused solutions made from individual plant flowers, each containing a specific imprint that responds in a balancing, repairing, and rebuilding manner to imbalances in humans on their physical, emotional, mental, and spiritual or universal levels."

I RESPECT NATURE AND HER ABILITY TO PREVENT ILLNESS AND TO PROMOTE HEALTH. THEREFORE, I USE THE ESSENCE OF FLOWERS TO SUSTAIN OR IMPROVE MY HEALTH.

PEACE & PROSPERITY ARE
MY DIVINE BIRTHRIGHT

What is your attitude about money? This is a big question. Have you been taught that money is evil? If so, why would you want any? Were you taught as a child that you can't afford things that you would like to have? Do you still tell yourself that you "can't afford" something when you go shopping? Is that old voice still playing in your head so it sabotages your ability to manifest abundance and prosperity?

Money is a form of energy. We are entitled to have abundance in our lives. It is our Divine Birthright. So why do so many people live in poverty or on the edge, just making enough to get by? I recently heard a newscaster say that sixty percent of Americans live paycheck to paycheck. That means families have no money in a savings account, no money for emergencies or for non-essential items like vacations. That means that the paycheck earners in the family, usually both parents, cannot be sick. They cannot *afford* to take time off, to be ill or to just rest, because their incomes are vital to the well-being of the household. That pressure is detrimental to a person's physical, mental and emotional health.

Peace of mind is essential to all aspects of our health and well-being. If you stay worried about earning enough to support your family, you can see how peace and prosperity are tied together. In fact, they are two sides of the same coin, inextricably bound together. As long as there are *the haves and the have-nots* in our world, there will be divisiveness. Peace depends on everyone having enough and having enough depends on peace prevailing. Wars are fought by one group seeking control over another and allocating resources in a manner that maintains the illusion that the group in power is deserving of wealth while the others are not.

This attitude of entitlement is under the surface; it is a belief that someone is worthy of prosperity, while others are not. This is a distortion of a fundamental truth. Self-esteem is healthy - self-aggrandizement is not. Boasting and bragging are not the expressions of mature individuals. People who have lots of money have *prosperity consciousness*, but that does not indicate a healthy sense of self-esteem; in fact, their attitudes can indicate other areas of immaturity such as disrespect for others and a willingness to take advantage of their positions of authority to get more, both power and money.

There are ways to improve your prosperity consciousness. Identifying old beliefs in lack and limitation is essential. Have you been told that rich people are unhappy or that being poor is a virtue? If these thoughts and beliefs are part of your pro gramming, your ego will defend them. Worse, this conditioning creates vulnerability to those who would exploit your feelings of unworthiness. Then your belief that you could be taken advantage of manifests as others profit from their own greed which often involves fraud, deceit and corruption.

It is your job to install new programs of abundance. This depends on your Higher Consciousness guiding you to know that you are worthy and deserving of prosperity. Having money is not evil nor will it make you unhappy. The thoughts of having wealth do not come from an ego programmed for poverty; they come from your true self who knows your inherent worthiness.

There are archetypes for prosperity. In the Goddess section of this book, we see Lakshmi, the Goddess of Good Fortune. Keeping her picture in your purse or in your home can remind you of this Divine Archetype. Attracting wealth is not a matter of luck, it is matter of mindset. What you think about, you create. If your subconscious mind is filled with thoughts that counter your conscious desire for affluence, your subconscious ego pro-gramming will win. If you feel you are more challenged now than ever, it is the perfect opportunity to experiment with putting new programs into your mind.

There is a legend of an Indian Grandfather, a wise elder, who is teaching his grandson about inner conflict. He tells the boy that there is a battle going on within him. He describes the conflict as if there is a pair of wolves, not just in him, but within everyone. One wolf has the attributes of peace, harmony, love, kindness, humility and more. The other wolf is full of rage, regret, greed, false pride and evil ways. Which one will survive? asks the boy. "The one you feed," replies his Grandfather. Ask yourself, which wolf are you feeding? Are you nurturing your belief in poverty or prosperity?

We have free will but we are bound by Universal Laws. The Law of the Circle, also known as the Law of Attraction, is one. Looking at the results you have in your life is a perfect way to assess the effects of your programming. If you have plenty, no problem. If you have less than you would like, now is the time to add new affirmations to your repertoire.

There is a balance of give-and-take that is based on the highest good for all concerned. When this balance is disrupted, as it has been for millennia, the few who control wealth can dominate and oppress those who buy into this distorted belief system. Those who are oppressed have lots of ego-evidence that they are not receiving a flow of abundance in their lives. What is challenging to understand is that this imbalance is a reflection of the deep inner programming that has prevailed for generations and is encoded in the cells of our brains and bodies.

Napoleon Hill wrote *Think and Grow Rich* in the 1930s. It became "one of the greatest best sellers of all time." Hill named six fears that are common: the fears of poverty, criticism, ill health, lost love, old age and death. The most common is the fear of poverty. He states that "fears are nothing more than states of mind." He describes six symptoms that demonstrate a fear of poverty: indifference, indecision, doubt, worry, overcaution and procrastination.

If you notice that you have this fear, the first step in attaining financial freedom is to clear your relationship with money. That means letting go of any fear that money is not your friend. It is a source of energy, and you are entitled to your share, in fact, an abundance. Even though world religions have preached that poverty and lack are the "Will of God," the opposite is true. Keeping the masses in fear and adhering to belief systems that serve to control them, perpetuates the disparity between our Higher Selves and our ego selves. Being poor is not virtuous. When we untangle the erroneous belief that our Creator would want His/ Her children to be poor, we can claim our Divine Birthright to be free of lack and limitation, and see ourselves in a new light ~ radiant Spiritual Beings having an earthly experience to remember who we are and how to cocreate with our Creative Source.

Check out your self-image. Are you still thinking in terms of your childhood conditioning which taught you that you were undeserving? Can you imagine yourself free of all the *rational-lies* you tell yourself about why you are not getting the best out of life? This means loving yourself, not thinking of yourself as bad, not good enough, or unworthy. You are actually denying yourself the best in life when you run these old programs over and over again. Your ego-mind believes what you tell it, even if it is not true.

Your thoughts and the words you use are significant. If you say you are worried about paying your bills, for example, your obedient mind will focus on your *worry* as the objective. The focus becomes what you *don't* desire instead of what you do, and your energy and attention flow in the wrong direction. Plus, the word *want* is a deal breaker. To be *in want* is to be totally lacking, to be in a state of deprivation. Stop wanting and start having. It begins in your mind, with what you think and what you say. Remember that scriptural admonition: "I shall *not* want?" When you unite with your Higher

Presence, your ego can stop holding you hostage to old beliefs that do not serve you. You *know* that prosperity is flowing toward you.

Start thinking in the positive. When will the check arrive? A sign of prosperity can show up at any moment ~ a gift, a discount, a prize. When will the new job or promotion manifest bringing you increased resources? Do your job well, envision doing a superb job or start by volunteering ~ giving away your services can provide new opportunities to feel good about yourself, meet helpful people and make a difference in the lives of those less fortunate than yourself.

Stop apologizing for desiring money. Stop worrying *and* hurrying. Hurrying can cause mistakes and accidents. Rushing can impede your concentration and cause inattention while worrying is total sabotage!

Use your inner vision to envision (in-vision) how you will feel when you *are* prosperous. What clothes will you wear, where will you live? Focus your *intention* and your *attention* on how good you will *feel*. Act as if prosperity has already arrived! You are creating a new blueprint for abundance. Think about gratitude and appreciation. Pray and meditate on all that you are grateful for. Smile!

Gratitude opens the door for the flow of abundance. In addition, giving *and* receiving keeps that revolving door open. If we desire money, we must give away money. Making donations to your favorite causes ~ with no expectation of getting anything back ~ paradoxically, catalyzes a return of energy, *magnified*, to you. What you have sent out with love and good will returns amplified. The Law of the Circle never fails!

Release all traces of poverty thinking. A tool that many are using to transmute negative programming is known as the Violet Flame. When you balance the pink light of your feminine qualities with the blue light of your masculine qualities, just as they blend on an artist's palette, these hues merge to become violet. Imagine this purple light surrounding every thought, word, feeling, action, belief and memory you have ever misqualified so that negativity disappears in the Light, transforming into luminous primal energy. Free every electron of your beautiful body from the clouds of negativity that have engulfed it. Envision the glorious violet flame of transmuting energy to nullify a lifetime of detrimental contamination so that you are a Goddess of Freedom!

> **I AM BASKING IN THE GOLDEN LIGHT OF PEACE AND PROSPERITY.**

> **I AM THE REAL DEAL.**
>
> **I ENVISION IDEALS,**
>
> **THEREBY, PREVENTING ORDEALS.**

I AM A GODDESS OF WEALTH

I AM A GODDESS WEARING A JEWELED CROWN.

A GOLDEN CROWN STUDDED WITH GEMS
OF BRILLIANT COLORS ENCIRCLES MY HEAD.

THESE JEWELS REPRESENT THE ATTRIBUTES
OF A DIVINE BEING WHO HAS AGREED TO SERVE
THE EARTH AND ALL HUMANITY IN
A PHYSICAL BODY
THIS LIFETIME.

I ALLOW THE COSMIC VIBRATIONS
OF THESE RADIANT HUES TO FLOW
IN, THROUGH AND AROUND ME.
I KNOW THAT EACH QUALITY
IS AN ASPECT OF MY BEING
WHICH I CAN EXPRESS HERE ON EARTH.

I SHARE MY INFINITE LOVE
WITH EVERYONE I ENCOUNTER,
RADIATING TO THEM MY ACKNOWLEDGEMENT
OF THEIR DIVINE PERFECTION.

THIS PRACTICE HOLDS THE SPACE
FOR EACH INDIVIDUAL TO BE THE BEST
THEY CAN BE.

I SEE THE HEALTH, BEAUTY AND TRUTH
OF WHO EACH PERSON IS,
THEREFORE, PERFECTION EMERGES
FROM THEIR HIGHER SELF,
WHO ALSO WEARS A JEWELED CROWN
OF INFINITE PERFECTION.

IN OUR ONENESS, WE GIVE THANKS. NAMASTE.

**I INVOKE THE PEACE THAT PASSES ALL
UNDERSTANDING**

I SURROUND EVERY THOUGHT, WORD, FEELING,
ACTION,
BELIEF AND MEMORY I HAVE EVER EXPRESSED
WITH THE VIOLET LIGHT
OF TRANSMUTATION.

I QUIETLY REFLECT ON WAYS THAT I CAN
IMPROVE THE QUALITY OF MY LIFE
BY HARMONIZING THE FEMININE AND MASCULINE
POTENTIALS WITHIN ME.

I AM DIVINE WILL.
I AM DIVINE WISDOM.
I AM DIVINE LOVE.

WHAT I DESIRE FOR MYSELF
I DESIRE FOR ALL HUMANITY.

I KNOW THAT AS I EXPRESS
THE HIGHEST AND BEST
FOR ALL CONCERNED,
GOODNESS RETURNS TO ME.

I EXPERIENCE PEACE BEYOND COMPREHENSION.

I AM ON PURPOSE IN MY LIFE WITH
JOY & ENTHUSIASM

Some of the greatest wisdom shared by avatars like Indian Spiritual Master Meher Baba is "Don't worry, be happy." Even songwriter and singer Bobby McFerrin, wrote "Don't worry, be happy. In every life, we have some trouble, but when you worry, you make it double. Don't worry, be happy."

However, if your childhood and, thus, your early programming taught you that life was sad, threatening, joyless, or otherwise dark and miserable, it is not just hard to be positive and happy, it can feel impossible. When your neural networks were forming, when each neuron was growing, the receptors on the cell membranes (think cell-brains) were predominantly those that perceived unhappiness. There were next-to-no receptors that perceived positive, loving or happy impressions. So now the idea of being happy can feel like a lost cause.

I used to joke that if my father had a motto it would have been: "If you're happy, you just don't understand the problem." Dad's mother died when he was one year old and his father and stepmother were harsh and demanding. He left home at 18 and eventually became a policeman, then a Security and Law Enforcement Officer in the United States Air Force. He felt it was his job to protect my mother and me; Mom could be happy, but life was serious and happiness was frivolous. I bless him now when I recall how he experienced so much pain in his life. Nonetheless, I modeled after him as all things male were of value in my family of origin. I got the good *and* the bad. I have to choose to be happy because joy and happiness do not come naturally to me.

Spiritual teacher Patricia Cota-Robles says that happiness "is a vibratory action which we must cultivate and practice through our Free Will choice every day." I have learned this very late in life, waiting for happiness to arrive unbidden or as a result of my circumstances. We can *cultivate* happiness by monitoring our thoughts, feelings, memories, beliefs and actions, keeping watch for those that lead to anger, rage, depression or despair. Then we can make an effort to find a positive thought, a joyful emotion, a happier memory, a revised belief system or a kinder action.

It can be a revolutionary idea to choose to be happy, or at least stop any negativity from weighing down our hearts and minds. Psychologist J. Martin Kohe wrote in 1953: "THE GREATEST POWER THAT A PERSON POSSESSES IS THE POWER TO CHOOSE." Among all the examples he gives is the power to *choose happiness*. If someone experiences happiness and then says, as many do, "this is too good to last," the sabotage has begun and the obedient subconscious mind will find a way to make happiness vanish!

The poet Rumi wrote: "Absorbed in this world you've made, it is your burden. Rise above this world. There is another vision." Writing this book has been such an adventure. It seems that every topic, every Goddess, every quality I address has had a lesson for me personally. I am learning to walk my talk and see that other "vision."

Dr. Wayne Dyer, motivational speaker and author of *Real Magic*, said: "A true barometer of intelligence is an effective, happy life lived each day and each present moment of every day." Now we begin to see that being *on purpose* in our lives does not just lead to happiness. It is not the way to happiness; being on purpose *is* our happiness.

Dr. Dyer had this vision:

When you are at purpose you are truly flowing with life, experiencing a kind of harmony that comes from not having to strive for something else. In short, you lighten up, figuratively and literally. This comes from the new knowing that enables you to go about your life's work free of worrisome thoughts. You sense that you are being watched over, and your actions come from this inner beatitude of rightness or correctness. When you are acting out of that inner knowing which constantly reminds you that you are on purpose and that you trust yourself to act out of that purpose, the right thing is all that you can do.

Dr. Dyer concurs with Patricia Cota-Robles calling unhappiness a habit that we can break by choosing happiness. The answer to creating lives of joy and happiness, according to Dyer, is to connect with our inner "invisible" selves. He is referring to our Higher Selves, the True Self that knows better than our limited egos.

Cota-Robles emphasizes, *"there is no permanent Happiness for any Lifestream until we finally Heal our self-inflicted separation from our own God Presence, 'I AM.'"* Our Higher Self is known by many names and when it "is once again in command of our vehicles [our bodies], our thoughts, feelings, memories and actions will reflect and accept our Purpose and reason for Being."

Leaders in the realm of spiritual thought suggest that we can connect with our Higher Selves and recognize the ego conditioning that continually keeps us focused on insatiable sensory gratification. There is never enough to satisfy those cravings. Real satisfaction is derived from finding our purpose and sharing our gifts with others.

To clarify your purpose and to experience more joy and happiness create a mind map or chart that defines your goals in the major areas of your life. Don't limit yourself in any way. Envision the best and most that you can. Let your inspirations guide your aspirations. When you have an inspiration to do something, even if out of the ordinary, write it down! State your goal as if it is already accomplished!

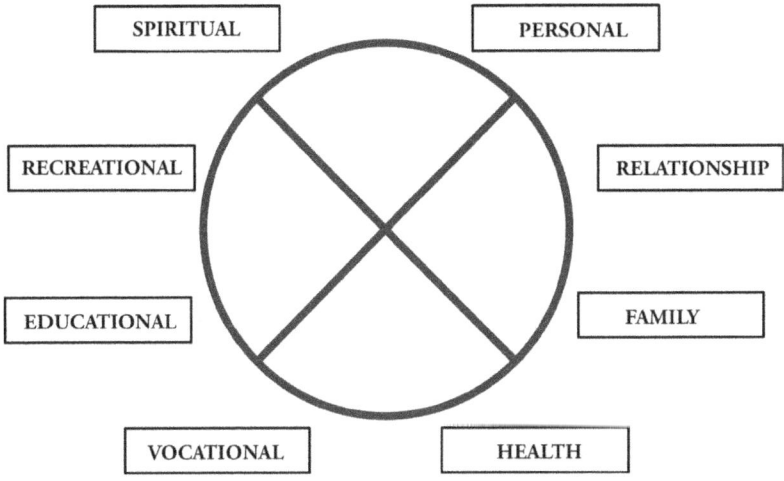

When you are exploring your purpose, ask yourself what you truly desire. Your purpose will be in areas of life that you enjoy and generates feelings of happiness and enthusiasm. You might feel a sense of exhilaration when you contemplate doing things you really like to do. You might find the image of Freya driving her chariot pulled by two cats humorous. Laughter is an expression of joy. Find de-Light (I love puns!) in all you do.

Challenges may confront you as you pursue your goals. These are not insurmountable impediments. As we practice a new attitude of acceptance and choose happiness we may encounter circumstances that we can view as either *obstacles or opportunities*. For example, working on this portion of the book, I wrote enthusiastically for a couple of hours ~ and I forgot to save periodically. Somehow my AutoSave button had been turned off so when I started creating a chart, I hit a button that caused my word document to disappear. In the past I would have had a hissy fit. This time I practiced what I preach, took a break and came back later.

It seems that there are lessons for me everywhere, even in writing ~ maybe *especially* in writing ~ because these are concepts I intend to share with others.

These ideas have developed over the course of my life, now over 80 years. I was learning about programming and affirmations in the 1980s. I longed to go to college, something I had not been able to do because of other choices I had made to marry and have children. In 1987, after my father died, I let go of a real estate career and spent the next four and a half years earning a BA and MA. I was 52 when I completed those degrees, earning a scholarship along the way. Through an amazing combination of serendipitous circumstances I ended up feeling empowered enough to earn a PhD at age 62. I loved going to school and when people told me I couldn't accomplish my goals or that it would be drudgery to write a thesis or dissertation, I chose subjects that I enjoyed and actually relished during the time it took to do the research and write up the results. I made collages, journaled and continued reprogramming myself. I recited affirmations and engaged in rigorous self-examination throughout my coursework.

I am learning to accept responsibility for all the happenings in my life. The Dalia Lama offers good advice: "When you think everything is someone else's fault, you will suffer a lot. When you realize that everything springs only from yourself, you will learn both peace and joy."

THE MIRROR OF LIFE

THE CIRCUMSTANCES IN MY LIFE MIRROR MY CONSCIOUSNESS.

MY HAPPINESS IS NOT DUE TO CHANCE.

MY HAPPINESS IS DUE TO THE CHOICES I MAKE,

AND I AM HAPPY EXERCISING MY FREEDOM TO CHOOSE.

**I AM ON PURPOSE IN MY LIFE.
I RADIATE THE PEACH LIGHT OF JOY AND HAPPINESS.**

I NOW KNOW THAT

**"WHEN I BELIEVE IT,
I WILL SEE IT."**

**MY HQ ~ MY HEALTH QUOTIENT ~
IS ALSO MY HAPPINESS QUOTIENT.**

**AS I FREE MYSELF FROM WORRY
AND FOCUS ON MY PURPOSE IN LIFE,
HAPPINESS SPONTANEOUSLY
OVERFLOWS.**

**MY HEART IS JOY-FULL
AND I EXPERIENCE VIBRANT HEALTH.**

"I AM" HAPPINESS

Through the Power of God, blazing in my heart, I offer myself as a conductor of God's Limitless Happiness and Joy into the world of form.

I invoke every part of Life which has ever contributed to the Cosmic Fount of Happiness and Joy since the beginning of time to come forth now and pour the Flame of Happiness through me to bless all Life evolving on the sweet Earth.

Blaze the Flame of Happiness and Joy through all the physical, etheric, mental and emotional substance on Earth, until all is raised into the embrace of God's Heart.

Illumine each part of Life with the Wisdom and Understanding that according to their ACCEPTANCE of this precious gift, will it manifest daily in their Life experiences.

I dedicate myself now to be the perpetual open portal through which the full-gathered momentum of God's Happiness and Joy will flow to bless all Life Eternally.

It is done! So be It! "I AM."

Patricia Cota-Robles, 1989

I AM TRANSFORMING MY LIFE

Transformation is about CHANGE! Most people are *change-averse*. An ego does *not* want to change so it will keep you stuck in old dysfunctional patterns of thought, feeling and behavior for a lifetime, unless you make a conscious effort to do something different! Transformation is about rebirthing, revitalizing and realizing potential. You can shift your consciousness and lift your spirit so that your life changes into one of enduring satisfaction.

To assist in achieving that goal, I rely on fairy tales. I love fairy tales, myths and stories that exemplify principles ~ truths ~ about who we are and what our potential really is. One modern tale is *The Wonderful Wizard of Oz*. This story was written by Frank Baum in 1900, but it is the 1939 movie, *The Wizard of Oz*, that really established the story as a classic, one that virtually everyone knows.

The story is about Dorothy, one of my heroines and an archetype that can awaken every woman to know her innate Goddess. Dorothy is knocked out during a tornado. While unconscious she enters a dream world that has characters in it that are part of her everyday physical reality, but in the dream they act out an adventure as parts of Dorothy that need recognition. These fellow travelers overcome challenges and ultimately Dorothy learns to appreciate what she already has ~ both within herself and in her outer reality. It is the realization of her inner qualities that is the focus of my interpretation of the story.

One way to interpret dreams is to perceive each of the characters as part of the dreamer. It is almost impossible *not* to do that when we look at Dorothy and her companions. First, her house lands on "the wicked Witch of the East" and kills her. Fairy tales often contain images of death and destruction. A good Witch appears and encourages Dorothy to journey to the Emerald City and seek the help of the Wizard of Oz. A second witch, the wicked Witch of the West, appears in a cloud of smoke and threatens Dorothy. She must relinquish the red slippers that were worn by the Witch of the East. There is no remorse, indeed, there is great celebration, because the wicked witch is dead!

So the story begins with encounters with witches, frightening beings that could represent hidden parts of Dorothy's persona. We have no background, but we could question what happened in her early childhood that brought her to live with her aunt and uncle? A sense of abandonment or rejection might have had a house topple onto it, clearing the way for more feelings of acceptance and love.

As Dorothy travels down the yellow brick road ~ a metaphor, a golden path to enlightenment ~ she first encounters a scarecrow. This charming being regrets not having a brain but is the smartest one of the troupe as he cleverly finds approaches to solve a variety of problems. The second fellow is a tin man who thinks he has no heart. Yet he is a feeling individual who shows signs of loyalty and devotion. The third figure is not a person but a lion, a symbol of courage. Each of these travelers question whether they have a brain, heart or courage, but all the qualities of intelligence, compassion and bravery are demonstrated during their quest.

The Wizard turns out to be a fraud, the classic "man behind the curtain." He barks loudly but is really a timid fellow trying to uphold an image he feels he can't embody. The contrast of bombast and reticence illuminate aspects of Dorothy's personality. Dorothy had all she needed on her journey to begin with: a brain, heart, and courage. She learned to appreciate staying in her own backyard; she was endowed with those great qualities from the beginning. We sense that being grateful for who we are is in our best interests, not seeking outside ourselves. In her desire to save the scarecrow, Dorothy threw water ~ a healing element associated with emotions ~ on the wicked Witch of the West and melted her. This frightening character was simply "liquidated," as the Wizard noted. Perhaps rituals, meditations and other healing modalities can transform our fear and pain into Light, at least light heartedness.

It is amazing to witness how our superconscious minds solve issues in our lives and do so with kindness and benevolence. The Wizard awarded each facet of Dorothy's inner being with something that signified to her deeper consciousness the recognition that the treasures were present within her originally, not earned later.

When Dorothy was rendered *unconscious,* she entered a slow brain wave state. When dreaming, unconscious while sleeping for example, our brains are vibrating at twelve cycles per second or less. Since the 1950s dreaming has been thought of as Rapid Eye Movement (REM) time. You can learn to access slower brain wave states and doing so allows you to reprogram (transform) old patterns and beliefs.

Hypnosis is a way to access this state but there are ways to do this yourself. Dr. Dorothy Gates created *SpectraDynamics* to teach individuals to do just that. Since her demise the program has been updated and brought to the internet as *Presence of Mind LLC*, which explains the rationale for reprogramming and how to easily and gently accomplish this.

Carl Jung said that "the privilege of a lifetime is to become who you truly are." He believed that our unconscious minds direct our lives without our conscious awareness, and that dreams can serve as a portal into the unconscious where we can experience "the myths forgotten by the day." David Rosen, a Jungian analyst, states: "transformation means to change the nature of our personality [ego]."

This often involves the "union of opposites," resolving a paradox. Transformation "can lead to the manifestation of our true self. We then can accept that we are here for a special purpose: to fulfill our own personal myth."

DREAM JOURNALING

I purchase a beautiful journal or make one of my own.

Each morning I take time to recall what I dreamt while asleep. Each dream has meaning.

I allow myself to wonder what meaning there is for me.

I draw pictures or find photographs that represent my dreams and place them in my journal.

When I counsel I frequently use a technique called Eye Movement Desensitization and Reprocessing (EMDR). I studied in the early 1990s with Francine Shapiro who developed the method. I have found it to be extraordinary as a client-centered technique for accessing healing and insight without interference from me as the therapist. My experience has shown me that clients access an alpha state of consciousness, that is a slower brain wave state, by moving their eyes. In that state they can experience thoughts, sounds, or bodily sensations that provide feedback or entirely new perspectives regarding the focus of their attention. Clients have experienced ah-ha moments, epiphanies that might otherwise never have occurred. It is amazing and a joy to behold as individuals find their own answers to situations that may have haunted them for years.

EMDR is a highly regarded process for dealing with trauma. I have watched individuals find understanding and relief from the trauma of incidents that had left such overpowering images of horror in their minds that it impacted their lives for years. When a person is in an alpha brain wave state, their subconscious minds and physical bodies are accessible literally at a cellular level. Bessel Van Der Kolk, who therapeutically addresses trauma and endorses EMDR as an effective modality, titled his outstanding book on the subject, *The Body Keeps the Score: Brain, Mind, and Body in the Healing of Trauma*.

Most people do not have such severe trauma memories stored in their minds and bodies. A more common example of difficulties that you could address with this method might be feeling disrespected at work. If coworkers have been derisive and you feel denigrated, you could deal with this issue with EMDR. At the end of your session you could begin to feel more confident or self-assured. While moving your eyes (I like to have clients move their eyes up-and-down to align their spines as they would in meditation) you may have a memory that reveals where and when you first felt disrespected by others, usually in early childhood. You might have an insight into what others have felt that makes them behave in a disrespectful manner. That awareness could help you view others with more compassion or consideration. When you are complete, repeating your affirmations, again while slowly moving your eyes up and down, locks in the new thoughts and feelings that counter the original complaint.

If this process appeals to you, please seek a counselor who is skilled in EMDR. However, eye movements occur naturally every night when you sleep. This is a time when your mind processes information. To illustrate how this works, you might feel achy and tired and say to yourself, "I'll feel better in the morning," and, sure enough, you do. Even without prompting, your mind will process the events of the day, categorizing, organizing, and filing information. Your dreams could help transform a frightening situation into an act of heroism on your part.

Here are some directions for deliberately moving your eyes with an intention in mind.

MOVING MY EYES

I take some time for myself. I sit quietly and think about the challenges I have been facing. I identify an objective, for example, I would like to feel better about a particular situation. I would like to understand more about how or why this situation occurred. I would like relief from my discomfort.

I create several affirmations that state the opposite of what is disturbing me. Some choices might be: I AM LOVED. I AM SAFE. I AM FREE. I AM TRUSTING. I AM TRUSTWORTHY. I AM RESPECTED. These are first-person statements that convey the message that these qualities are already mine.

To begin my eye movements, I find a vertical surface like the edge of a door or the intersection of two walls meeting in a corner. I move my eyes up and down. I count eleven or more repetitions. I pause, close my eyes, take a deep breath and identify a thought, an emotion or bodily sensation that occurred as I moved my eyes. When I have a new image or feeling, I move my eyes vertically again. I repeat the eye movements for no longer than 20 minutes. I ask myself if I am ready to repeat my affirmations. Ready or not, I repeat them and give thanks.

You can experiment with eye movements to deal with issues that come up for you. You could sit in your chair at the office, turn your face to a corner where you can align your eyes and, without anyone knowing, you could move your eyes up and down following the vertical intersection of two walls. That seam just gives you a guide for your eyes to follow. Think about what has occurred and create an affirmation to counter the event: I AM respected; I AM at ease; I AM calm. These statements give your mind and body the message that the desired outcome is not just possible, it is already accomplished. If I have not said it before, your subconscious mind is your obedient servant and will create what you tell it to. It does not know the difference between what is imagined and what is real. This process could work for you. Accessing your subconscious mind in this manner can be life-changing.

Stories and myths of transformation abound. Hans Christian Andersen's tale of *The Ugly Duckling* is another classic. The movie *Hans Christian Andersen* starring Danny Kaye tells this story in a charming way. A child who is teased by other children gets the message that he will become ~ transform into ~ a swan, a metaphor many of us would have appreciated hearing when we were little.

In our myth of Isis, the Goddess represents rebirth, restoration, renewal and resurrection. It is our job to find these attributes within ourselves. Transforming our childhood programming changes our past! Perhaps a good way to begin is to use butterfly imagery. This is an image that is frequently employed to describe the alchemical process a caterpillar goes through to become an entirely different creature ~ a butterfly. I heard Joan Borysenko describe this process in one of her presentations. This is truly transformation!

Transformation is change and change is inevitable. The famous quote attributed to Greek philosopher Heraclitus is "The only constant in life is change!" You can expect to change and you can shape the changes in yourself by letting go of old programs stuck in your biocomputer and installing new ones. Change can occur as a situation to do what you have always done or a change could provide an opportunity to do something different according to the new programming you are placing in your biocomputer. Spiritual teacher Patricia Cota-Robles points out that those who resist change:

Are experiencing a "grinding of the gears" literally the "screaming and gnashing of teeth." This is causing excruciating pain, and it is being reflected in every aspect of Life—finances, health, relationships, careers, physical, mental, emotional and spiritual well-being. In order to eliminate the pain, we must *let go* of the old programming, concepts and beliefs of the past that are keeping us stuck.

I can now simply affirm that my reaction is often not how I want to behave, it is not even a response that is part of who I am. "Not me, not mine."

Changing the past is an intriguing idea. It is not what happened in the past but how we perceived what happened. Since the mind does not know the difference between what is real and what is imagined, painting a new vision on the canvas of our minds can imprint a new set of beliefs, especially about ourselves and how others treat us. We see ourselves in a new light. We see that whatever happened, it can contribute to our Divine Purpose and how we share our experiences and insights with the world.

Joan Borysenko, an innovative psychotherapist and prolific author, shared in her book *Minding the Body, Mending the Mind*, that if you are "truly motivated to become free from past conditioning," the process of accomplishing this goal is "not realized in the reading of one book or many." Your process is one of "gradual unfolding." She calls this:

A process of gradual unfolding—a gentle awakening rather that a storming of the citadel by force. Like anything of value, self-awareness flows best when nurtured with respect and attention. It's human nature for attention to wander and to seemingly forget things that have been learned. Yet, since all these learnings are stored within the mind, and since new learnings spring from the Self, they can never be completely forgotten. Changes in attitude and understanding may come forward at any time and in ways that surprise and delight you. Be assured that the efforts you have already made will continue to enrich you. Keep your heart and mind on the goal, and go easy with yourself along the way. The goal is closer than you might think.

> **I CHANGE THE THINGS ABOUT ME THAT I CAN.**
>
> I ACCEPT THE THINGS I CANNOT CHANGE, THOSE THINGS THAT ARE THE RESPONSIBILITY OF OTHERS.
>
> I SEE IN THE MIRROR OF LIFE MY OWN BELIEFS ABOUT ME.
>
> I HAVE THE WISDOM TO DISCERN THE DIFFERENCE BETWEEN CAUSE AND EFFECT.
>
> I TAKE RESPONSIBILITY FOR MY THOUGHTS, FEELINGS, WORDS AND ACTIONS SO THAT THEY TRULY REFLECT WHO I AM.

We know that love has a transforming effect. David Hawkins says:

> The crucial point is: by changing ourselves, we change the world. As we become more loving on the inside, healing occurs on the outside. Much like the rising of the sea level lifts all ships, so the radiance of unconditional love within a human heart lifts all of life.

As we begin our transformation we become more aware. Our consciousness expands. We know our Oneness with all Life including the Earth beneath our feet and the Heavens above. We can honor our connection to the Elements by envisioning the Light that each of the elements emits and declaring our Oneness with that Light.

Our Life Journey is enriched by our expressions of appreciation for the Air we breathe, the Earth we walk upon, the Fire which warms us, the Water we drink and that bathes us, and the Ether which ever encompasses our bodies.

HONORING THE ELEMENTS

I ENVISION A GLOBE OF GOLDEN LIGHT SHINING ABOVE MY HEAD. THIS REPRESENTS THE ETHER ELEMENT AND MY CONNECTION TO THE HEAVENLY REALMS, AND I REPEAT "I AM."

WITH EVERY BREATH I TAKE I ENVISION A SAPPLHIRE BLUE LIGHT RADIATING AT MY THROAT. THIS REPRESENTS THE AIR ELEMENT, AND I REPEAT "I AM THE BREATH OF THE CREATIVE SOURCE."

I ENVISION A CHRYSTALLINE PINK LIGHT FILLING MY CHEST. THIS REPRESENTS THE FIRE ELEMENT, AND I REPEAT "I AM THE HEART OF THE CREATIVE SOURCE."

I ENVISION AN OPALESCENT LIGHT PULSING AT THE BASE OF MY SPINE. THIS LIGHT SIGNIFIES THE WATER ELEMENT AND I REPEAT, "I AM THE HARMONY OF MY EMOTIONS."

I ENVISION A RUBY RED LIGHT GLOWING AT MY FEET. THIS REPRESENTS THE EARTH ELEMENT, AND I REPEAT "I AM THE MASTER OF MY PHYSICAL LIFE."

Your greatest gift is knowing your own WORTH. As you value the Elements that support and sustain you, repeat this affirmation:

> ## I AM A BEING WORTHY OF ESTEEM.
> ## I AM A PRECIOUS CHILD OF THE CREATIVE SOURCE.

Spiritual teacher Patricia Cota-Robles says:

> To change from a consciousness of low self-esteem and unworthiness to the acceptance of our True God Reality often seems like an impossible task, but in fact, it is just a SLIGHT ADJUSTMENT IN AWARENESS. Remember, the separation from our God Presence is self-inflicted. It is a result of years of distorted programming and erroneous beliefs. Our God Presence is ALWAYS patiently awaiting our return to Truth. It is but a breath away, and our acceptance of this knowledge is all that is necessary for this part of our true Being to take command of our four lower bodies.

Joseph Campbell, a wise and eloquent professor who taught comparative mythology and religions, said before his passing in 1987: "All I can tell you about mythology is what men have said and have experienced, and now women have to tell us from their point of view what the possibilities of the feminine future are." Margaret Starbird said in *The Woman with the Alabaster Jar*, "the resurrected feminine consciousness will continue to move toward equal partnership in spite of the myth of the dominant male that has been perpetuated for millennia." You, in all your glory, are transforming the world with its old worn-out ideas into a brand new world with a bright future that moves humanity from a paradigm of fear to a paradigm of Love.

**I AM ENGULFED IN THE LUMINOUS OPAL LIGHT
OF TRANSFORMATION.**

I adapt and change easily,
improving the quality of my life.
As I do so, the lives of everyone on the planet
are uplifted as well.

What I wish for myself
I wish for every man, woman and child.
May all the Goddess qualities I express
also shine from within each person on Earth.

EPILOGUE

I would like to share some profound words written for young girls ~ and all of us ~ by authors and songwriters that I admire. Here is *Self-Esteem* by brilliant therapist Virginia Satir.

SELF ESTEEM

By Virginia Satir
1970

I am me.
In all the world, there is no one else like me.
There are persons who have some parts like me,
but no one adds up exactly like me.
Therefore, everything that comes out of me
is authentically mine because I alone chose it.
I own everything about me,
my body, including everything it does;
my mind, including all its thoughts and ideas;
my eyes, including the images of all they behold;
my feelings, whatever they may be
anger, joy, frustration, love, disappointment, excitement;

my mouth, and all the words that come out of it,
polite, sweet or rough, correct or incorrect;
my voice, loud or soft;
and all my actions, whether they be to others or to myself.
I own my fantasies, my dreams, my hopes, my fears.
I own all my triumphs and successes,
all my failures and mistakes.
Because I own all of me,
I can become intimately acquainted with me.
By doing so I can love me
and be friendly with me in all my parts.
I can then make it possible for all of me
to work in my best interests.

I know there are aspects about myself that puzzle me,
and other aspects that I do not know.
But as long as I am friendly and loving to myself,
I can courageously and hopefully
look for solutions to the puzzles
and for ways to find out more about me.
However I look and sound,
whatever I say and do,
and whatever I think and feel
at a given moment in time is me.

When I review later
how I looked and sounded,
what I said and did,
and how I thought and felt,
some parts may turn out to be unfitting.
I can discard that which is unfitting,
and keep that which proved fitting,
and invent something new from that which I discarded.

I can see, hear, feel, think, say, and do.
I have the tools to survive,
to be close to others,
to be productive,
and to make sense and order out of the world
of people and things outside of me.
I own me, and therefore I can engineer me.
I am me and I am okay.

THE TRUTH ABOUT YOU

A QUOTE FROM OUR FATHER-MOTHER GOD

By Patricia Cota-Robles in *The Bigger Picture*

"You are a precious and Beloved Child of God. Your unique Golden Thread of Life confirms your Divinity and reveals the reality that you are an essential part of Earth's Ascension in the Light. This knowing will renew your faith in yourself and will remind you that you are a priceless Human Being. Once this realization truly registers in your heart and your conscious mind you will never again say 'What good could I possibly achieve?' 'What value am I?' 'What difference will one soul make?' *You will recognize those words to be a sacrilege.*

We are your Father-Mother God. We created you and we have chosen to express some beautiful manifestation of Life through you. You are destined to fulfill a portion of the glorious Divine Plan unfolding on Planet Earth. Now is the time for you to release the unique perfume and music of your Being to bless all Life. The Purity of your individual fragrance and keynote is unlike any other ever released by the evolving Sons and Daughters of God. Something sacred is hidden within your Being that has never been known by another. It is an exquisite expression of Life which your I AM Presence alone can externalize. It is time for you to accept this Divine Truth. It is time for you to stand revealed as your mighty I AM Presence grown to full stature. And so it is."

In a world where change is the only constant, it is a blessing to remember that we are children of the Creative Source ~ and that will never change.

YOU CAN RELAX NOW

Song and Lyrics by Shaina Noll
You can relax now.
C'mon and open your eyes.
Breathe deeply now.
I am with you.

Oh, my sweet, sweet child,
who do you think you are?
You are the child of God
and that will never change.

You had a dream. You misunderstood.
You thought we were separate,
but now you hear my voice, and
you can relax now.
C'mon and open your eyes.
Breathe deeply now.
I am with you.

You are the love of my life.
You are my one creation.
You are eternity,

and that will never change.

You can relax now.
I am with you.
You are the child of God,
and that will never change.

You can relax now.
You are the child of God
and that will never change.

REFERENCES

A Course in Miracles. https://en.wikipedia.org/wiki/A_Course_in_Miracles

Allen, J. (no date). *As a Man Thinketh.* Grosset & Dunlap.

As within, so without. https://www.goodreads.com

Austen, H. I (2018). *The Heart of the Goddess.* Monkfish Book Publishing.

Baum, L. F. (2019-2023). *The Wonderful Wizard of Oz.* Seawolf Press.

Benson, H. (1975). *The Relaxation Response.* Avon Books.

Biles, S. (July 30, 2024). *NBC News.*

Bonheim, J. (1997). *Goddess: A Celebration in Art and Literature.* A Fairstreet/ Welcome Book.

Borysenko, J. with L. Rothstein. (1987). *Minding the Body, Mending the Mind.* Addison-Wesley Publishing.

Brandon, N. (1992). *The Power of Self-Esteem.* Health Communications, Inc.

Brandon, N. (1983). *Honoring the Self.* Bantam Books.

Brandon, N. (1969). *The Psychology of Self-esteem. Bantam Books.*

Briggs, D. C. (1970). *Your Child's Self-Esteem.* A Dolphin Book.

Britannica. https://www.britannica.com

Butler, A. B. (2009). Triune brain concept: A comparative evolutionary perspective. *ScienceDirect.* https://www.sciencedirect.com/science/article/abs/pii/B9780080450469009840

Campbell, D. (1991). *Music: Physician for Time to Come.* Quest Books.

Campbell, J. (2013). *Goddesses: Mysteries of the Divine Feminine.* New World Library.

Cashford, J. (1993). *The Myth of Isis and Osiris.* Barefoot Books.

Center on the Developing Child. Harvard University. developingchild@harvard.edu.

Chamberlain, D. (2013). *Windows to the Womb*. North Atlantic Books.

Chamberlain, D. (1988). *Babies Remember Birth*. Jeremy P. Tarcher, Inc.

Chitty, J. (2013). *Dancing with Yin & Yang*. Polarity Press.

Chopra, D. https://www.deepakchopra.com/about/

Cogentinfo.com/resources/the-impact-of-social-conditioning-on-womens-leadership

Confucius. https://www.open.edu/openlearn/education/12-famous-confucius-quotes-on-education-and-learning

Cota-Robles, P. (2019). *The Bigger Picture*. Waterside Productions.

Cota-Robles, P. (1994). *Stargate of the Heart*. New Age Study of Humanity's Purpose.

Cota-Robles, P. (1989). *The Next Step*. New Age Study of Humanity's Purpose.

Cumes, C., & Valencia, R. L. *Pachamama's Children*. (1995). Llewellyn.

Dalai Lama. https://www.goodreads.com/quotes/7290558-when-you-think-everything-is-someone-else-s-fault-you-will#:~:text=When%20you%20think%20everything%20is%20someone%20else's%20fault%2C%20you%20will,learn%20both%20peace%20and%20joy.

Davis-Floyd, R., & Arvidson, P. S. eds. (1997). *Intuition: The Inside Story*. Routledge.

Dossey, L. (1999). *Reinventing Medicine: Beyond Mind-Body to a New Ear of Healing*. HarperSanFrancisco.

Dyer. W. W. (1997). *Manifest Your Destiny*. HarperCollins.

Dyer, W. W. (1995). *Your Sacred Self*. HarperCollins.

Dyer, W. W. (1992). *Real Magic: Creating Miracles in Everyday Life*. HarperCollins.

Dyer, W. W. (1989). *You'll See It When You Believe It*. Avon Books.

Einstein, A. artsandculture.google.com/story/who-really-said-these-5-famous-phrases/JAXh1xsiCEHOqw?hl=en

EMDR Institute. https://www.emdr.com

Era of Peace. https://eraofpeace.org

Findeisen B. https://starfound.org/

Forgiveness. https://greatergood.berkeley.edu/topic/forgiveness/definition

Freya. https://skjalden.com/freya/

Gadon, E. W. (1989). *The Once and Future Goddess*. Harper & Row.

Gates, D. https://presenceofmindllc.com/about-us/

Gerhardt, S. (2004). *Why Love Matters: How Affection Shapes a Baby's Brain*. Routledge.

Ghandi, M. https://www.bbc.co.uk/worldservice/learningenglish/moving-words/shortlist/gandhi.shtml

Gottman, J. M. (2021). *The Science of Trust*. W. W. Norton & Co.

Grace. https://en.wikipedia.org/wiki/Divine_grace

Graham, G. (1994). *The One-eyed Man Is King*. Gordon Graham & Co.

Greeley, A. M. (1977). *The Mary Myth: On the Femininity of God*. The Seabury Press.

Hallam, E. (1996). *Gods and goddesses*. Macmillan.

Hasta pura. https://en.wikipedia.org/wiki/Laetitia

Hawkins, D. R. (1995). *Power Versus Force*. Veritas Publishing.

Hay. L. L. (1987). *You Can Heal Your Life*. Hay House.

Hayward, J. https://strangewondrous.net/browse/author/h/hayward+jeremy+w

HeartMath Institute. https://www.heartmath.com

Heline, C. (2010). *Healing and Regeneration through Color*. Kessinger Publishing.

Hendricks, G. (1982). *Learning to Love Yourself*. Prentice Hall Press.

Heraclitus. https://www.goodreads.com/author/quotes/77989.Heraclitus

Higher Self Yoga. https://www.higherselfyoga.org/what-is-the-higher-self

Highsmith, S. (2014). *The Renaissance of Birth: Changing the Language of Childbirth*. Words Matter Publishing.

Highsmith, S., Landsberg, C., & Vernallis, M. A. (2004). *Babies Know* (DVD).

Hildegard of Bingham. https://www.azquotes.com/author/21274-Hildegard_of_Bingen

Hill, N. (1966). *Think and Grow Rich*. Wilshire Book Company.

Holy Bible. King James Version.

Imperial News. https://www.imperial.ac.uk

Jung, C. https://www.goodreads.com/quotes/75948-the-privilege-of-a-lifetime-is-to-become-who-you

Kinsley, D. (1989). *The Goddesses' Mirror*. State University of New York Press.

Klaus, M. H., Kennell, J. H., & Klaus, P. H. (1995). *Bonding*. Perseus Books.

Kohe, J. M. (1953). *Your Greatest Power*. Combined Registry Company.

Lady Justice. https://en.wikipedia.org/wiki/Lady_Justice

Lakshmi. *The Goddess of abundance and beauty in you*. https://www.yogabali.com

Laughlin, C. (1997). In *Intuition: The Inside Story*, R. Davis-Floyd & P.S. Arvidson, eds. Routledge.

Levin. B. H. (2000). *Your Body Believes Every Word You Say*. Words Work Press.

Levin, V. (2003). National Institutes of Health, Bethesda, MD.

Lincoln, A. https://www.brainyquote.com/quotes/abraham_lincoln_100845

Lipton, B. (2005). *The Biology of Belief*. Mountain of Love/Elite Books.

Luke, H. M. (1981). *Woman Earth and Spirit*. Crossroad.

MacFarlane, R. (2016). *Mary and the Divine Sophia*. Greater Mysteries Publications.

March of Dimes. https://www.marchofdimes.org/

Matthews, C. (1992). *Sophia Goddess of Wisdom*. Aquarian/Thorsons.

Meher Baba. https://www.goodreads.com/work/quotes/690706-listen-humanity

Mayo Clinic. *Biofeedback*. https://www.mayoclinic.org/tests-procedures/biofeedback/about/pac-20384664

McCannon, T. (2015). *Return of the Divine Sophia*. Bear & Co.

McCarty, W. A. (2004)v. *Welcoming Consciousness*. Wondrous Beginnings Publishing.

McCourt, M. https://www.goodreads.com/quotes/40467-resentment-is-like-taking-poison-and-waiting-for-the-other

McFerrin, B. https://genius.com/Bobby-mcferrin-dont-worry-be-happy-lyrics

McGarey, G. (2023). The 'Well-Lived Life. Atria Paperback.

McWilliams, P. (1988). *You Can't Afford the Luxury of a Negative Thought*. Prelude Press.

Minett, G. (1994). *Breath & Spirit*. Aquarian/Thorsons.

Moberg, K. (2003). *The Oxytocin Factor: Tapping the Hormone of Love, Calm and Healing*. DA CAPO Press.

Mollenkott, V. R. (1983). *The Divine Feminine*. Crossroad.

Monaghan, P. (2014). *Encyclopedia of Goddesses and Heroines*. New World Library.

Monaghan, P. (1997). *The New Book of Goddesses & Heroines*. Llewellyn.

Monsay, E. H. (1997). In *Intuition: The Inside Story*, R. Davis Floyd & P. S. Arvidson, eds. Routledge.

Muten, B. (2003). *Goddesses: A World of Myth and Magic*. Barefoot Books.

Myss, C. (1997). *Why People Don't Heal and How They Can*. Three Rivers Press.

National Institutes of Health. https://www.nih.gov

Newberg, A. & Waldman, M. R. (2012). *Words Can Change Your Brain*. Plume.

Olson, C. (Ed.). (1988). *The Book of the Goddess Past and Present*. Crestwood.

Palmer, M., Ramsay, J. with Kwok, M-H. (1995). *Kuan Yin*. Thorsons.

Pearce, J. C. (1992). *Evolution's End*. HarperCollins.

Philip, N. (1995). *The Illustrated Book of Myths*. Dorling Kindersley.

Popova, M. *Einstein on Fairy Tales and Education*. https://www.themarginalian .org/2014/03/14/einstein-fairy-tales/

Phillips, R. (June 2013). The Sacred Hour: Uninterrupted Skin-to-Skin Contact Immediately After Birth. *Newborn and Infant Nursing Reviews*, *13*:2, 67-72. https://www.sciencedirect.com/science/article/abs/pii/ S1527336913000299

Pixabay. https://pixbay.com

Porges, S. W. (2011). *The Polyvagal Theory*. W. W. Norton.

Presence of Mind, LLC. presenceofmindllc.com

PSYCH-K Centre International. Psych-k.com

Rapp, R. (1997). Forward in *Childbirth and Autorotative Knowledge*, Floyd, R. D., & Sargent, C. F. Eds. University of California Press.

Regula, D. *The Mysteries of Isis*. Llewellyn.

Rigoglioso, M. (2010). *Virgin Mother Goddesses of Antiquity*. Palgrave MacMillan.

Rosen, D. H. (1993). *Transforming Depression*. Tarcher/Putnam.

Rothschild, B. (2000). *The Body Remembers*. W. W. Norton.

Ruether, R. (2005). *Goddesses and the Divine Feminine*. University of California Press.

Ruether, R. R. (1977). *Mary: The Feminine Face of the Church*. Westminster Press.

Ruz, D. M (1997). *The Four Agreements*. Amber-Allen Publishing.

Sadhguru. (2024). https://isha.sadhguru.org/us/en

Sanford, L. T. & Donovan, M. E. (1984). *Women & Self-Esteem*. Penguin Books.

Satir, V. (1975*). Self Esteem*. Celestial Arts.

Scaer, R. C. (2001). *The Body Bears the Burden*. Haworth Medical Press.

Schenker, D. (2007*). Kuan Yin: Accessing the Power of the Divine Feminine*. Sounds True.

Schore, A. N. (1994). *Affect Regulation and the Origin of the Self*. Lawrence Erlbaum Associates.

ScienceDirect. https://www.sciencedirect.com

Shakespeare, W. (no date). *Hamlet, Act III, Scene I*. https://poets.org/poem/hamlet-act-iii-scene-i-be-or-not-be

Shapiro, R. (2012). *The Divine Feminine in Biblical Wisdom Literature*. Skylight Paths Printing.

Siegel, D. J. (1999). *The Developing Mind*. The Guilford Press.

Spretnak, C. (1978). *Lost Goddesses of early Greece*. Beacon Press.

Starbird, M. (1993). *The Woman with the Alabaster Jar*. Bear & Co.

Starhawk. (1979). *The Spiral Dance: A Rebirth of the Ancient Religion of the Great Goddess*. Harper & Row.

Starhawk, Baker, D. & Hill, A. (1998). *Circle Round: Raising Children in Goddess Traditions*. Bantam Books.

Starr, R. (2015). *You Are Woman, You Are Divine: The Modern Woman's Journey Back to the Goddess*. Over and Above Press.

Steffen, P. R., Hedges, D., & Matheson, R. (April 2022). The brain is adaptive not triune: How the brain responds to threat, challenge, and change. *Frontiers in Psychiatry*, 13. www.frontiers in.org

Stone, M. (1976). *When God Was a Woman*. Harcourt.

Sunbeck, D. (2002). *The Complete Infinity Walk*. Leonardo Foundation Press.

Telesco, P. (1998). *365 Goddess*. HarperSanFrancisco.

Tipping, C. C. (2002). *Radical Forgiveness*. Global 13 Publications.

Van der Kolk, B. A. (2014). *The Body Keeps the Score*. Viking.

Verny, T. R. (2021). *The Embodied Mind*. Pegasus Books.

Verny, T. R. with J. Kelly. (1981). *The Secret Life of the Unborn Child*. Dell Trade Paperback.

Verny, T. R. with P. Weintraub. (2002). *Pre-parenting: Nurturing Your Child from Conception*. Simon & Schuster.

Walker, B. (1983). *The Woman's Encyclopedia of Myths and Secrets*. HarperSanFrancisco.

WebMD. https://www.webmd.com/brain/limbic-system-what-to-know

What is the Higher Self? https://www.higherselfyoga.org/what-is-the-higher-self

What Is Self-Regulation? https://positivepsychology.com/self-regulation/

Williamson, M. (1993). *A Woman's Worth*. Ballantine Books.

Wright, M. S. (1988). *Flower Essences: Reordering Our Understanding and Approach to Illness and Health*. Perelandra, Ltd.

www.ingramcontent.com/pod-product-compliance
Lightning Source LLC
Chambersburg PA
CBHW042315120626
46547CB00022B/2076